CITIZENS BUT NOT AMERICANS

Citizens but Not Americans

Race and Belonging among Latino Millennials

Nilda Flores-González

NEW YORK UNIVERSITY PRESS
New York

NEW YORK UNIVERSITY PRESS
New York
www.nyupress.org

References to Internet websites (URLs) were accurate at the time of writing. Neither the author nor New York University Press is responsible for URLs that may have expired or changed since the manuscript was prepared.

Library of Congress Cataloging-in-Publication Data
Names: Flores-González, Nilda, author.
Title: Citizens but not Americans : race and belonging among Latino millennials / Nilda Flores-González.
Description: New York : New York University Press, 2018. | Includes bibliographical references and index.
Identifiers: LCCN 2017008027| ISBN 9781479825523 (cl : alk. paper) | ISBN 9781479840779 (pb : alk. paper)
Subjects: LCSH: Hispanic American young adults—Race identity.
Classification: LCC E184.S75 F56 2018 | DDC 305.868/073—dc23
LC record available at https://lccn.loc.gov/2017008027

New York University Press books are printed on acid-free paper, and their binding materials are chosen for strength and durability. We strive to use environmentally responsible suppliers and materials to the greatest extent possible in publishing our books.

Manufactured in the United States of America

10 9 8 7 6 5 4 3 2 1

Also available as an ebook

To Elena, Diana, and Julian

CONTENTS

ACKNOWLEDGMENTS

As I put the final touches on this book, I cannot help but wonder how the young women and men who were interviewed for this project feel today—after Donald Trump was elected U.S. president despite a campaign that portrayed Latinos as a threat to the nation. I would not be surprised to find that more than ever they feel as *citizens but not Americans* but are also more than ever bent on claiming—and fighting for—their right to belong. I want to thank these young Latinos for sharing their stories. I hope that my analysis does justice to their words.

I am forever indebted to my colleagues Andy Clarno, Lorena Garcia, Michael Rodriguez-Muñíz, Maura Toro-Morn, and Steve Warner for reading drafts and providing comments that helped shape this book. I am particularly touched by Lorena Garcia's generosity in both time and kindness, and her insightful and always on-point comments. I am also indebted to Michael Rodríguez-Muñíz for helping me sharpen my arguments. This book was enriched by many lively conversations with Andy Clarno, Bradley Zopf, Jessica Cook, and Maura Toro-Morn that pushed me to further develop my ideas. I have been lucky to find a mentor and good friend in Steve Warner, an extraordinary scholar with a big heart who took me under his wing the day I arrived at the University of Illinois at Chicago, and who to this day continues to mentor me. Thanks to my writing buddy, Pamela Popielarz, for keeping me accountable and encouraging me through the different stages of the writing. I want to thank Ilene Kalish, Caelyn Cobb, and Alexia Traganas from NYU Press for their support and guidance. I also want to thank the anonymous reviewers for their constructive comments that help me improve the manuscript. My appreciation also goes to the undergraduate students who helped collect data for this project.

I want to express my gratitude to my dear friends Maura Toro-Morn, Mony Ruiz-Velasco, Monina Diaz, and Lisa Milam for keeping me sane and for providing much-needed laughter. In this long process, others provided support and encouragement: Susie Karwowski, Chris Bergin, Aixa Alfonso, Pamela Quiroz, Elizabeth Aranda, Héctor Cordero-Guzmán, Marisa Alicea, and Juanita Goergen. I am also grateful to my colleagues at UIC, who, like me, approach their work with a commitment to social justice: Xochitl Bada, Claire Decoteau, Tyrone Forman, Elena Gutierrez, Amanda Lewis, Patrisia Macias-Rojas, Amalia Pallares, Atef Said, Laurie Schaffner, and Nena Torres. Special thanks to Barbara Risman and Maria Krysan for their unwavering encouragement. Thanks also to Tara Williams and Jennifer Michals for their support throughout this process.

Lastly, I want to thank Joel Palka and our children, Elena, Diana, and Julian, for keeping me grounded and focused on what matters in life, and for motivating me to keep going when I was ready to give up. Elena, Diana, and Julian, I hope that you always know that you belong. And to my late father, Erving, my mother, Eva, and my siblings, Angie, Evi, Naydi, Machin, and Diani, thank you for always having my back.

1

Race and Belonging among Latino Millennials

Danila is a twenty-two-year-old second-generation woman of Mexican descent whose narrative provides a glance at Latino millennials' experiences as citizens but not Americans when she says:

> I don't think I am an American. I would say that I am Mexican because I think based on my experiences I would identify as a Mexican. Like when people look at me they are not like "Oh yeah, she's an American." When they see me they think "Oh yeah, she's Mexican." Society doesn't see me as an American. They see me as a Mexican. So I guess that's why I don't see myself as American, because others don't see me as an American. If they don't see me as an American, why should I see myself as an American?

Although Danila was born in the United States, her everyday experiences belie her status as an American. Her physical appearance marks her as Mexican and erases her Americanness. Her experiences underscore the role of race in notions of belonging to the American imagined community. Danila is not alone. Feeling that they are citizens but not Americans is the underlying theme I found in my research on second- and third-generation Latino millennials.

Why does it matter that these youths feel excluded? We should pay heed to what these Latino millennials say because, by sheer numbers, they will inevitably have a significant social, economic, and political impact on U.S. society. Latinos are the second-largest racial group, and Latino millennials specifically constitute one-fifth—and the second-largest segment—of the millennial population. As the largest generational cohort of Latinos in U.S. history, these youths—who in 2017 range in age from twenty to thirty-six—will propel the Latino population exponentially as they have children over the next two decades. Yet, we do not know much about Latino millennials beyond basic demographics, save for a few educational studies that point to their dim prospects for social mobility. The stories I present here tell how these U.S.-born children and grandchildren of immigrants from Latin America are becoming integrated into contemporary American society. In *Citizens but Not Americans*, I provide a deeper understanding of Latino millennials by examining how they understand race, experience race, and develop racialized notions of belonging.

I focus on race because in these youths' narratives it emerges as the most meaningful social category attached to notions of belonging. As an essential social marker, race defines who belongs to the American imagined community. Race is indisputably the common thread in these narratives and plays a central role in how these young people perceive themselves, the position they occupy in the U.S. racial order, and their status as members of the polity. In exploring the centrality of race in shaping notions of belonging among Latino millennials, I argue that current racial ideas and practices impact the ways in which this group understands race, makes meaning of lived experiences as racialized subjects, and develops racialized notions of belonging that are marked by racial exclusion. I show how multidimensional and intersecting processes of racialization are particularly pronounced as Latino millennials navigate their daily lives and their place within American society.

The narratives presented in this book reflect three distinct yet interrelated themes—*Latinos as an ethnorace*, *Latinos as a racial middle*, and *Latinos as "real" Americans*—that emerged from interviews with ninety-seven U.S.-born Latino youths in 2009. Their narratives capture their feelings of exclusion from the imagined American community along three dimensions—racial categorization, racial hierarchy, and national inclusion. Racialized along these three dimensions, these youths find themselves outside of the boundaries of how "American" is defined. Yet their narratives challenge their exclusion and push for their recognition as Americans. These three themes are illustrated in the narrative of a twenty-one-year-old second-generation Mexican named Arielle, whose words capture the essence of what the Latino millennials in this study experience.

Arielle

Arielle is a college student who lives in a predominantly Mexican neighborhood on Chicago's South Side. Her parents are immigrants from

Mexico who met in Chicago and have struggled to make a life for themselves and their children. Arielle likens her family's experiences to those of other minority groups. She explains:

> I am part of the working class. My parents do work hard, but they never had the luxury of being happy and saying, "Oh, I am middle class or upper class." [They are] only happy with just being able to have a house and being in the U.S. raising their kids [with] everyone in school. I feel like I am definitely part of the working class and part of a somewhat subordinate group. Because we are a majority, but we also don't get as much representation as people who are white or I think anyone who is not white [can] kind of relate to us because we are all in the same mix, [in] the same boat.

Being U.S.-born, Arielle has views on the American dream that differ from those of her immigrant parents. While her parents are content with what they have accomplished in comparison to their lives in Mexico—holding stable jobs, owning a house, sending their children to college—Arielle notices the inequities that mark her life as a racial minority in the United States and that prevent her from sharing the privileges enjoyed by whites. The limits of the American dream are apparent to Arielle, who believes that despite the fast growth of the population, Latinos' numerical majority does not translate to equality. She stresses that being a Latina, "it is like a constant struggle because even though we are growing and becoming a majority, even if the whole U.S. becomes half Hispanic, we will still be viewed as being beneath anyone who is white or American because just the fact [of] the history and the color of our skin." To her, Latinos will continue to stand out as nonwhite and non-Americans even if they reach a numerical majority. Implied in Arielle's words are the three themes—Latinos as an ethnorace, a racial middle, and "real" Americans—that characterize these millennials' narratives of belonging.

The idea of Latinos as an ethnorace—the first theme in these Latino millennials' narratives—illustrates how the exclusion of Latinos from conventional U.S. racial categories has eroded these youths' sense of belonging. Like Danila, Arielle is aware that based on her appearance, "people assume a whole list of things I could be," but white and American are not among them. Inverting the general usage of terms, Arielle identifies racially as Mexican American and ethnically as Latino and Hispanic. Like Arielle, the Latino millennials in this study found themselves in a racial quandary, knowing that they do not fit in the white or black racial categories that are imposed on them, but also do not have an officially recognized racial category to claim as their own. Yet they assert racial labels that are meaningful to them as well as to others. In the absence of an official racial category, they appropriate ethnic and panethnic terms such as "Mexican" and "Hispanic/Latino" as racial referents. This seemingly inconsistent racial identification pattern among the youths reflects a problematic racial categorization scheme based on abstract notions of race that do not align with how people think about, experience, or practice race in everyday life.

My analysis reveals that these youths conceptualize themselves as an ethnoracial group (see Alcoff 2006). Their ethnoracial categorization includes racial and cultural attributes about what makes up the stereotypical Latino, such as "tan" skin color, Spanish language, particular foods and music, family values, and Latin American ancestry. Arielle identifies skin color as a visible marker of her ethnoracial status when she says, "Being a Mexican American, either way I am not white, I am still a different color skin from someone else that automatically like singles me out and stuff." In addition to physical traits, Arielle points to ancestry and culture as additional markers of her ethnoracial status when she states, "I think if you are of any kind of Latino or South American descent, you know, if you can speak Spanish or you know someone in your family is from a country that speaks Spanish or something, that makes you that [Latino]." These youths understand that to others, and to themselves, they constitute a separate ethnoracial group made up of people of Latin American ancestry, even when this is not officially recognized. Having no proper designation in the U.S. racial scheme, and feeling forced to choose from racial categories (e.g., white or black) that do not befit them, Latino youths find that their racial miscategorization leaves them with a diminished sense of belonging.

The second narrative—Latinos as racial middle—is rooted in the youths' sense of marginalization derived from their subordinate status in the racial hierarchy. Just as they do not fit in conventional racial categories, these youths do not fit in a racial order characterized by a sharp color line that places whites at the top and blacks at the bottom, and that assumes that Latinos fit on one or the other side of the color line. Not fitting within these conventional racial categories, Arielle believes that Latinos "fall in the between, [in] the gray area," because they are "viewed as being beneath anyone who is white or American." Like Arielle, many other millennials understand themselves as occupying an "intermediate" or "racial middle" social position that is lower than that of whites but higher than that of blacks.

My findings challenge the assumption that Latinos are "becoming white" and are therefore situated closer to whites in the racial hierarchy. These millennials' narratives show that they do not locate themselves at the upper end of the racial hierarchy alongside whites, but neither do they locate themselves at the very bottom with blacks. Theirs is a racial middle that tilts toward the lower echelons of the racial hierarchy—much closer to blacks' subordinate status than to whites' superior status. Arielle says, "I definitely feel closer to pretty much the African American or other like Hispanic ethnicity. I feel like we are all kind of viewed as one big kind of group of people, that since we are not white we are automatically viewed as not bad but not good for the country or something. I can relate to that because we are all in the same boat in the end trying to fight to be equal to everybody else." Latino millennials in general felt closer to—and had a sense of solidarity with—blacks, with whom they share a marginal status, as well as with Middle Easterners, particularly those with Arab and Muslim backgrounds.

In contrast, these youths feel distant from Asians and whites mainly because they generally have much less interaction with people from these groups. But by far those they feel most distant from—and those they perceive as occupying a privileged position in the racial hierarchy—are whites. Arielle distances herself from whites when she says, "I definitely feel different from the American, you know, white people and a few Asians simply because they haven't had to go through the struggle we had growing up and as a grown-up they also have an upper hand you know. . . . I don't think they will ever truly know what it's like to live the life that we do. They have not always had it easy, but they had that extra push." Like Arielle, these youths' self-location in the bottom half of the racial hierarchy is based on both structural and everyday racialized experiences that mark them distinctively as nonwhite. These struggles make them question their status as Americans and differentiate them from whites and Asians, whom they view as occupying an advantageous position.

The last theme—Latinos as "real" Americans—speaks to the youths' struggle to insert themselves within the boundaries that define who is American. Despite their birthright citizenship, upbringing, and socialization into American culture, these youths are reluctant to call themselves Americans. This reluctance sprouts from their ethnoracial exclusion—or not having the racial and cultural traits required to be seen as full-fledged members of the American imagined community. Using familiar American tropes, these youths offer a counternarrative that challenges their ethnoracial exclusion and demands inclusion on their own terms.

Like most of the Latino millennials interviewed for this study, Arielle understands herself as a citizen mainly because, as she says, "I was born here, I have my papers straight, they've been straight since birth." For Arielle, birthright or naturalization is the determinant for citizenship. Yet she falters when asked how she understands herself as an American. She responds, "When I think of the term 'American,' the first thing I think of is like any person being born in the U.S., or actually any Caucasian or white person who is being raised in this country all their life on American values from back in the day, pretty much . . . I think technically anyone who is born in the U.S. will be American." While "technically" an American is anyone born in the United States, there are racial (white), cultural (values), and generational (from back in the day) criteria to being American that Arielle does not meet. Arielle states that "the only reason why I fit into this definition is because I am Mexican American because obviously I am not 100 percent Mexican. I was not born in Mexico, but since I was born in the U.S. that makes just the term, just a label of American, but I am Mexican because that's what both of my parents are, and that is how I was raised." Although she is technically American, Arielle uses the term "Mexican American" to denote that she is U.S.-born of Mexican descent. Like Arielle, those youths who identify in this way do so to distinguish themselves from their foreign-born counterparts.

Being othered as noncitizens and non-Americans, these youths develop an awareness and an understanding of the limits of citizenship and Americanness. Although they are citizens by birth, they are aware that they are seen by non-Latinos as noncitizens because their Latin American ancestry—disclosed by their looks, cultural manners, and/or surname—points to their immigrant background. Conjectures about their immigrant roots call into question their legality, as others assume that anyone who is "Latino" must be undocumented. Arielle faces the stigma of "illegality" in everyday life, such as when "the student who never experienced other races automatically thought that my family, you know, had a lawn-mowing business, or they thought they were illegal, and that was not true." She adds, "When I encounter people who are against immigration and they see that I am Mexican or Latino or Hispanic descent, they view me as 'You people are always coming here illegally' or they automatically think that I am an immigrant or I am here illegally or my family are related to being illegal, and they do not see the whole story." These racialized experiences erode Arielle's sense of belonging and lead her to form a pragmatic view of belonging that stresses legal rather than cultural membership in the American imagined community.

In *Citizens but Not Americans*, I examine the effect of racialization on Latino millennials' understanding of their marginal status in U.S. society. Ancestry, skin color and phenotype, social class, education, gender, language, and aspects of culture converge and shape how these youths experience and navigate everyday racialization. Racialized along three dimensions—as an ethnorace, as a racial middle, and as not "real" Americans—these youths remain outside of the boundaries of "American." Identifying as citizens but not Americans belies their status as full members of U.S. society and points to the entrenchment of race in notions of belonging to the American imagined community. My purpose in writing this book is to contribute to our understanding of Latino millennials' place in U.S. society, and particularly of how they make sense of themselves as Americans. To understand why these youths feel they are citizens but not Americans, we need to examine how they come to understand and define themselves as such.

Race as a Social Construct

In examining how these youths come to understand and define themselves as citizens but not Americans, I use a social constructionist theoretical framework. Like Omi and Winant (2014), I view race as a fundamental organizing principle in U.S. society, but one that is socially constructed. This approach posits that race has no factual scientific biological basis and that its relevance is due to the social meaning given to physical or phenotypic characteristics. Through the process of "race making," people are "othered," or made different, based on their physical features, but this "othering" also includes cultural traits. In "othering," a group's presumed physical and cultural characteristics are essentialized and believed to be endemic. Racialization happens when racial meaning is given to a group, and that group's categorization is created and re-created in social interactions and structures.

As Omi and Winant (2014) pose, race is ubiquitous in that it is embedded in individual and institutional social relations and in the social, economic, political, and cultural structures that permeate everyday life. The perniciousness of this racial social system lies in its quotidian and increasingly elusive nature with a popular discourse on color blindness that underplays the continuing significance of race. Bobo and Smith (1998) argue that the systematic, overt, and violent racism that characterized the Jim Crow era has been replaced by gentler laissez-faire racism. Likewise, Bonilla-Silva (2003, 2013) argues that this post–civil rights racism is characterized by the rearticulation of racism in seemingly imperceptible and covert ways. Today's racism is manifested in the repeated and frequent discrimination that happens in everyday life (Bonilla-Silva 2003, 2013; Essed 1991; Feagin and Cobas 2014) and that is manifested in what Pierce et al. (1978) have labeled *racial microaggressions*. These everyday "put-downs" directed at a person or group are intended to exclude and marginalize racial groups as inferior and undesirable (Pierce et al. 1978). As is apparent in ideologies, policies, and practices that disadvantage nonwhite people in order to protect white privilege, race has real and definite social consequences for different racial groups (Bonilla-Silva 2003, 2013; Omi and Winant 2014).

In the United States, race is characterized by a sharp color line that divides whites and blacks, and a racial hierarchy that parallels the distribution of and access to resources. This color line is closely guarded by clearly demarcated racial boundaries that are policed in informal and formal ways by individuals, institutions, and the state. While individual policing takes the form of prejudice and discrimination, institutional and state policing of racial boundaries involves unequal access to resources, as well as legalized and institutionalized forms of surveillance, profiling, confinement, incarceration, and violence directed at racial minority groups (Omi and Winant 2014). The institutionalization of Latino racialization permeates Latinos' daily life experiences and impacts their life chances.

In this book, I unpack the process of "race making" by examining how Latino millennials experience "othering" in everyday life and how these experiences shape their understanding of themselves as marginal members of the U.S. polity. While staying firmly grounded in sociology, I use an interdisciplinary approach that borrows concepts developed by political scientists, historians, anthropologists, philosophers, and legal scholars to examine the centrality of race to young Latinos' understanding of themselves and their social positions. I also use an intersectional lens to unravel the complexities of Latinos' self-understandings that lead to a diminished sense of belonging to the national community. In simple terms, intersectionality examines the ways that various forms of discrimination, oppression, and privilege act together. It also draws attention to the obvious and not so obvious connections between different social categorizations such as race, gender, sexuality, legal status, and social class. While each of these social categorizations individually increases or decreases chances for discrimination, when they are combined, the chances and impacts of discrimination may magnify or lessen. Intersectionality purposely engages in linking social categorizations to uncover how particular connections—or configurations—minimize or accentuate social articulations such as racial identification. An intersectional approach thus provides the critical means—and the analytical power—required to identify how members of the same group experience racial dynamics differently, and are impacted differently, due to their specific locations within interlocking systems of oppression.

Although I draw on an intersectional approach to guide my analysis of the experiences that youths articulated in their interviews, its application is not always obvious because many of these young people's experiences were a matter of degree rather than kind. I made an intentional effort to apply an intersectional lens whenever the data permitted, allowing me to make note of those instances in which the collusion of race, gender, legal status, and/or social class had an effect on the frequency, intensity, and type of racial experiences as well as the youths' responses to these experiences. These approaches—interdisciplinary and intersectional—allow me to develop a more complex understanding of how race is conceptualized and experienced by U.S.-born Latino millennials. By identifying and untangling the multidimensional process of racialization, I show how intersecting forms of exclusion lead Latino youths to develop subjectivities that signal their marginal status in U.S. society. By understanding how Latino millennials are racialized, we can gain insights into why these youths feel that they are citizens but not Americans.

The Racialization of Citizenship and Americanness

This book is grounded in Castles and Davidson's (2000) notion of *citizens who do not belong*. Castles and Davidson argue that there are citizens whose ethnic, racial, or religious backgrounds highlight their cultural differences and limit their access to the rights and privileges of citizenship. They pose that belonging to the nation-state requires both political and cultural membership. Political membership is based on documentation such as birthright or naturalization and imparts civil, political, and social rights to its bearers. Cultural membership is based on cultural homogeneity—manifested in shared values and ideals—such that assimilation is required in order to belong. Thus, there can be citizens who, despite their political membership, do not enjoy all the rights of citizenship because of "cultural" exclusion based on race, ethnicity, class, gender, or religion. They are what historian Mae Ngai (2007) calls the *alien citizen*, describing them as citizens by birth whose immigrant ancestry, discernible by racial and cultural traits, marks them indelibly as foreigners and renders their status as citizens and Americans dubious. By having their political and cultural membership questioned, these groups are positioned outside the boundaries that define who is a citizen and an American. That is, they are otherized as noncitizen and non-American.

Ngai's notion of the alien citizen is tied to the racialization of U.S. citizenship and American national identity as white. As whiteness became the prerequisite for becoming both a citizen and an American, those defined as nonwhite were deemed foreigners, unassimilable and banned from access to naturalization (Carbado 2005; Haney Lopez 2006; Ngai 2007). As a result of the racialization of citizenship and Americanness as white, nonwhite groups continue to be imagined as foreigners as this label extends to subsequent generations (Carbado 2005; Jiménez 2010; Ngai 2007; Tuan 1999). Alienage is then a *permanent condition* (Ngai 2007), and these groups remain *forever foreigners* (Tuan 1999) and *permanent immigrant groups* (Jiménez 2010) despite their historical presence and long-standing status as U.S. citizens. As their marginalization endures through the generations, minority groups come to define themselves collectively through their exclusion (Castles and Davidson 2000). Although I use the phrase "citizens but not Americans" to describe the Latino millennials' feelings of exclusion from the American imagined community, this phrase conveys the notion that these youths are both *citizens who do not belong* and *alien citizens*.

To understand why Latino millennials feel they are citizens but not Americans, we need to review the social, political, and historical processes involved in the construction of Latinos as citizens who do not belong and alien citizens. These processes were under way by the time of the annexation of Mexican territory in 1848 and the colonization of Puerto Rico in 1898, which construed the inhabitants of these territories—and those of Mexican and Puerto Rican national origin—largely as white and thus eligible for citizenship. The Treaty of Guadalupe Hidalgo stipulated that U.S. citizenship would be extended to Mexican citizens of the annexed territory. Puerto Ricans were also largely defined as white because, as Duany (2002, 247) argues, in a society that defined itself as white, classifying the Puerto Rican population as mostly white "helped to allay the common racist fear that the U.S. government had annexed a predominantly black population after the War of 1898." While these populations were defined largely as white for citizenship purposes, they were not commonly understood as white. As historians and legal scholars show, being "white by law" made Mexicans eligible for citizenship, but socially they remained nonwhites (Almaguer 2008; Gomez 2007; Haney Lopez 2006; Menchaca 2002; Molina 2014). That is, in everyday life, they were treated as nonwhites. Scholars add that in common understanding and practice, Mexicans occupied a social position distinct from whites, blacks, Asians, and American Indians (Almaguer 2008; Menchaca 2002; Molina 2014). Marked by their ethnicity, which distinguished them from other (European-descent) whites, Latinos remained a "race apart" or "off-white" (Almaguer 2008; Gomez 2007; Hayes-Bautista and Chapa 1987; Menchaca 2002). These notions applied to Puerto Ricans and subsequently to all Latin Americans—they were citizens by law, but certainly they were not Americans by common understanding.

Paradoxically, Latinos' "whiteness" was a basis for what legal scholar Devon Carbado (2005) calls *inclusive exclusion*. Carbado argues that groups defined as nonwhite or non-American occupy a position of racial liminality that renders them simultaneously as insiders and outsiders. He likens this racial liminality to being "foreign in a domestic sense." He argues that groups experience inclusive exclusion when they encounter exclusion from citizenship, exclusion from the imagined American community, and/or exclusion from equal rights and opportunities. Latinos can be described as experiencing inclusive exclusion. As "white ethnics," Latinos had access to citizenship and some of its perks, but their ethnicity became the basis for exclusion from Americanness and from the full rights and privileges of citizenship. As Fox and Guglielmo (2012) put it, Latinos were *boundary straddlers* because in some instances they counted as whites, and in others they were considered nonwhite. That is, sometimes they were included, and at other times they were excluded. Latinos often deployed their whiteness in claims making to gain access to resources such as citizenship, voting rights, and white schools, but their ethnicity was in turn used to deny them full access to other rights and privileges. While black exclusion was based on their assumed racial inferiority, Latinos' exclusion was based on their assumed cultural inferiority. In other words, blacks were excluded because they were not white, and Latinos were excluded because they were culturally inferior "whites." Regardless of its basis, both groups' exclusion involved their legal and social separation from whites. For instance, Mexicans' segregation into all-Mexican schools and classrooms was based not on the legal separation of races, since Mexicans were considered "white by law," but on their presumed linguistic and cultural differences (MacDonald 2004; Valencia 1991). Mexicans' whiteness was also the basis for differential justice as a jury of non-Latino whites constituted a jury of peers in cases where the defendant was Mexican (Haney Lopez 2004). Mexicans and Puerto Ricans also counted as whites in integration efforts. As Fernandez (2012) shows, racial integration in Chicago's public housing was achieved by counting Mexican and Puerto Ricans as whites.

In the early twentieth century, Latinos' exclusion expanded beyond assumed cultural inferiority as their citizenship status increasingly came into question. By 1924, this exclusion was embodied in what Molina (2014) calls an *immigration regime*, which redefined Mexicans, and by extension all Latino groups, not only as immigrants but also as undocumented. It was at this time that the U.S.-Mexico border became problematized as the source of unauthorized immigration, leading to the creation of the Border Patrol and the enactment of border enforcement. This assumed illegality extended to U.S.-born Mexicans, many of whom were deported along with Mexican nationals during the 1930s and again in the 1950s (Ngai 2004). In the 1990s, the Border Patrol deployed three initiatives to deter unauthorized immigration from Mexico. Operations Hold the Line, Gatekeeper, and Safeguard led to the extension of the fence separating the United States and Mexico, increased surveillance along the border, and accelerated processing of those crossing without authorization. Along with border and immigration enforcement came other measures aimed at curbing the growth of the Latino population, such as the involuntary sterilization of Mexican and Puerto Rican women (Chavez 2013; Gutierrez 2008; Lopez 2008) and a push to deny public services and assistance to undocumented immigrants in California through Proposition 187 (Hayes-Bautista 2004; Perea 1997). Most damaging were a series of federal laws that increasingly restricted immigrant rights and extended immigration enforcement. More recently, there has been promotion of English-only legislation, attempts to dismantle birthright citizenship from children born to immigrant mothers who are dubbed "anchor babies" (Chavez 2013; Ngai 2007), and recent local laws that criminalize Latino immigrants (Varsanyi 2010).

The legacy of the racialization of citizenship and Latinos' status as alien citizens is manifested today in the public perception of Latinos as "immigrants," "foreigners," and "illegals" (Oboler 1995; Omi and Winant 2014; Rosaldo 1997; Rosaldo and Flores 1997). "Illegal immigrant" has also come to mean "Mexican" and is often applied to anyone who looks Mexican regardless of legal status or ethnic/national origin (Chavez 2013; DeGenova 2005; Oboler 1995; Omi and Winant 2014; Rosaldo 1997; Rosaldo and Flores 1997; Santa Ana 2002). These images and assumptions spill into the U.S.-born Latino population and mark its members also as immigrants and "illegals." My previous work on youth participation in the immigrant rights marches of 2006 and 2007 shows that U.S.-born youths participated due to their racialization as "illegals" (Flores-González 2010). Despite their citizenship, they continue to be marked as alien citizens, with both their citizenship and their Americanness challenged.

The illegalization of Mexicans, and its extension to Latinos, has been accompanied by the construction of Mexicans—and Latinos in general—as the most serious threat to American society (Chavez 2013; Santa Ana 2002). The "brown scare" likens Mexican immigration to invaders who threaten to destroy the American way of life (Santa Ana 2002). Historian Samuel Huntington (2004) exemplified this anti-Latino sentiment when he argued that Mexicans, and other Latinos, are unassimilable because they refuse to adopt the Anglo-Protestant-based American creed and culture and continue to segregate themselves culturally, geographically, and economically. To him, the persistence of Mexican ethnicity will be "the end of the America we have known for more than three centuries" (Huntington 2004, 45). Huntington ignores the sociohistorical processes and structural factors that define "Americans" as white and Anglo-Saxon, that shaped and continue to shape the cultural, geographic, and economic segregation of Latinos, and that deny Latinos recognition and full rights as members of the polity. The "Latino threat" has refueled the immigration regime, leading to the militarization of the U.S.-Mexico border, a record number of deportations under President Barack Obama's administration, and calls for deportation without hearings for unaccompanied minors caught crossing the border. The Latino threat also powered Donald Trump's campaign call to "Make America Great Again" by painting Mexican immigrants—and by extension all Latinos—as "illegals," criminals, and rapists and pushing for an increase in deportations and the building of a wall to seal off the U.S.-Mexico border. This rhetoric has led to the construction of undocumented immigrants as undeserving, and because Mexicans—and other Latinos—are singled out as the "illegals," this image casts a shadow on U.S.-born Latinos in terms of their citizenship and Americanness. It is in this sociohistorical context that Latino millennials construct notions of national belonging.

The Hispanic and Latino Category

A prominent feature in the otherization of Latinos as citizens but not Americans is their classification as a panethnic rather than a racial group. Their historical racialization as legally white but socially nonwhite stressed their cultural rather than racial difference from whites, paving the way for panethnicity to emerge. Despite national origin, racial, class, linguistic, cultural, gender, and legal status differences, the term "Hispanic" homogenizes people of Latin American ancestry based on their assumed common heritage and shared cultural traits, particularly the Spanish language. Research on Hispanic/Latino panethnicity explores three articulations of panethnicity: institutional, communal, and individual. Recognizing these three strands is essential to understand why Latino millennials embrace panethnic identification along with national origin identification and often use both as proxies for race.

First, the institutionalization of Hispanic/Latino panethnicity is due to three different organizational actors who in collusion, but for their own interests, helped to formalize it as an official category, and led to its acceptance and widespread use as a descriptor for people of Latin American descent. In *Making Hispanics*, Cristina Mora (2014b) poses that the grouping of Latinos under the Hispanic panethnic category responded to political, social, and economic interests by three institutional actors: the state, Latino activists, and the media. The state's early attempts to identify the Latino population relied on reporting of foreign birth or parentage, Spanish language spoken at home, or Spanish surname. As a result, many Latinos who were of a third or subsequent generation, did not speak Spanish, or did not have a Spanish surname (as a result of marriage or intermarriage) were not identified as part of the Latino population (Chapa 2000). In the era of civil rights, the need to accurately count and identify Latinos intensified (Chapa 2000), and the federal government—prompted by Latino activists—adopted the term "Hispanic" as the legal designation for people of Latin American ancestry (Hattam 2007; Mora 2014b).

Recognizing the economic, social, and political interests at stake with the passing of civil rights legislation, Latino activists pushed for, and embraced, the state's Hispanic panethnic categorization and efforts to more accurately count this segment of the population (DeSipio 1996;

Mora 2014a; Oboler 1992, 1995). Other grassroots activists rejected the state's imposition of the term "Hispanic" due to its direct association with Spain and its colonial legacy in the Americas and joined the panethnic movement by coining and adopting the term "Latino" (Calderon 1992). Rodríguez-Muñíz (2015) contends that national civil rights organizations, regardless of which term they adopted, engaged in the politics of demography by supporting the enumeration of the Latino population to justify their claims for legitimacy and political power. What followed was the evolution of cultural, social, and political single national origin organizations into panethnic organizations (Itzigsohn 2009; Mora 2014b; Ricourt and Danta 2002). In *The Trouble with Unity*, Cristina Beltran (2010) argues that Latino panethnicity gives the illusion of a unified Latino political body with common political interests and policy agendas. The challenge of Latino unity, then, lies in how to bring together people who are perceived to share cultural characteristics but who sometimes hold different political ideologies and agendas.

In concert with the state and Latino activists, the media and the advertising industry's branding and marketing of Hispanics for general consumption or as a niche market also contributed to the labeling, homogenization, and institutionalization of Latinos as a distinct panethnic group (Mora 2014b). Scholars argue that the media creates and re-creates an "unaccented," "sanitized," and "whitewashed" Latino identity free of intraethnic rivalry by downplaying national origins and renationalizing them as Hispanic or Latino (Dávila 2008; Mora 2014b; Rodriguez 1997). Dávila (2001) argues that these "unaccented" images brand and label Latinos as a distinct (and foreign) group rather than normalizing them as part of U.S. society. Dávila (2001, 2008) further argues that commercial representations of Latinos, although skewed, contribute to the development of a cultural identity among Latinos that ultimately distinguishes them from whites but also from other minorities with whom they share experiences of racialization.

Second, the basis for the institutionalization of Hispanic/Latino panethnicity rested on the emotional connections felt by Latinos of different national origins. Early panethnic sentiment was grounded on the similar cultural, social, and political experiences, as well as the common experiences of migration, discrimination, and low socioeconomic status that Latinos encountered in the United States, yet the development of these connections was limited by the historical concentration of Latino subgroups in different regions of the country (DeSipio 1996). Growing diversity and dispersal of the Latino population has resulted in increased contact between Latino groups, leading to what Ricourt and Danta (2002) call *experiential panethnicity*, or daily interactions between Latinos of different national origins who mingle in families, neighborhoods, school, work, and churches. These *convivencias diarias*, or daily-life experiences, strengthen ties and solidarity between groups (Itzigsohn 2009; Pérez 2003; Ricourt and Danta 2002; Rodríguez-Muñíz 2010; Rúa 2001). As these groups interact, structural differences take a backseat as commonalities become more salient. Ricourt and Danta (2002) argue that proximity and daily interaction lead to the development of *categorical panethnicity* as Latinos come to see themselves as part of one larger group. This sense of Latinidad emerges from the affective ties that form through daily interaction, yet it does not develop at the expense of national origin identities. That is, panethnic and national origin identities coexist (Garcia and Rúa 2007; Ricourt and Danta 2002).

Third, the communal sense of Latinidad that emerged through daily interactions, paired with the increasing institutionalization and popularization of panethnic labels, led to the individual adoption of panethnic identification among Latinos. Studies show that although Latinos identify primordially by national origin, there is a significant increase in those who identify panethnically as Hispanic or Latino, particularly among younger cohorts (Hitlin, Brown, and Elder 2007; Oboler 1992; Portes and Rumbaut 2001; Telles and Ortiz 2008). Fraga and colleagues (2010) found that a "supermajority of respondents" strongly identified with panethnic labels while strongly identifying by national origin too. Scholars argue that panethnic labels are "addenda" or secondary identities that are neither instrumental nor an expression of solidarity; rather, they are all-purpose identities to which Latinos grow attached and identify with in addition to national origin (Itzigsohn 2004; Itzigsohn and Dore-Cabral 2000; Jones-Correa and Leal 1996; Oboler 1992; Telles and Ortiz 2008). They add that Latinos hold a multiplicity of identities simultaneously and that these identities are not mutually exclusive and thus provide them with identity options to select from, or activate, in different contexts depending on the type of interaction and with whom, where, and when it takes place (Fraga et al. 2010; Itzigsohn 2004;

McConnell and Delgado-Romero 2004; Rodriguez 2000; Schmidt, Barvosa-Carter, and Torres 2000). Recent research points to the racial connotations of panethnic labels as shown in their increased use for racial identification (Dowling 2014; Flores-González, Aranda, and Vaquera 2014; Flores-González 1999; Frank, Akresh, and Lu 2010; Hitlin, Brown, and Elder 2007; Itzigsohn 2004; Perez and Hirschman 2009; Roth 2012).

Factors such as nativity, language use, age, gender, education, religious affiliation, generation, discrimination, national origin, region, segregation, and skin color affect Latinos' identity choices (Campbell and Rogalin 2006; Eschbach and Gomez 1998; Golash-Boza 2006; Holley et al. 2009; Jones-Correa and Leal 1996; Perez and Hirschman 2009; Portes and Rumbaut 2001; Telles and Ortiz 2008). Taylor et al. (2012) found that nativity and language are the "strongest predictors of identity preferences" among Latinos. Foreign birth (and having foreign-born parents), living in the Southwest region, living in a predominantly Latino neighborhood, having Spanish spoken at home, having darker skin, and experiencing discrimination are factors that strengthen national origin identification (Portes and Rumbaut 2001; Taylor et al. 2012; Telles and Ortiz 2008). Panethnic identities are most common among native-born individuals who grew up after the civil rights movement, who speak Spanish at home, who live in a city with a large Latino population, and who have experienced discrimination (Campbell and Rogalin 2006; Masuoka 2006; Perez and Hirschman 2009; Telles and Ortiz 2008). In a study of second-generation adolescents of Latin America, Caribbean, and Asian origin, Rumbaut (1994) found that panethnic identification is higher among youths who are female, are native-born, are not affluent, are inner-city residents, and have experienced discrimination. These panethnic identities are also more common among those of mixed Latino origin (Aparicio 2016; Flores-González 1999; Rúa 2001).

Other studies show that panethnic identification is more marked among younger U.S.-born Latinos than among immigrants and older U.S.-born Latinos (Hitlin, Brown, and Elder 2007; Oboler 1992; Portes and Rumbaut 2001; Telles and Ortiz 2008). These intergenerational differences reflect these individuals' personal experiences growing up. Immigrants can summon a national identity based on their experiences growing up in their home countries, but those in the second generation have only their U.S.-based experiences. In addition to generational differences, there are cohort differences that account for younger Latinos' greater ease in identifying panethnically. These youths have grown up at a time when these terms are already institutionalized and are part of everyday life, making them more likely to embrace this identity.

The Chicago Context

The Chicago area, with its confluence of demographic, social, and political dynamics, presents a unique site for studying Latino identity, and particularly panethnicity among Latino millennials. For the past seventy years, Chicago has consistently held one of the largest concentrations of Latinos in the nation. With more than 2 million Latinos, the Chicago Metropolitan Area (CMA) now has the fifth-largest Latino population in the nation, and Cook County—where Chicago is located—ranks fourth in the nation (Brown and Lopez 2013). Latinos' share of the Chicago population grew from 14 percent to 28.9 percent from 1980 to 2010. The concentration of Latinos in suburban Chicago has precipitously increased in the past two decades. Attracted by job opportunities, Latin American immigrants, mostly Mexican, are bypassing the city and settling in these new suburban Chicago destinations, as well as exurban and rural communities farther from the city core. The suburbanization of Latinos was evident by 2004, when 54 percent of Latinos in the state lived in Chicago's suburbs (Ready and Brown-Gort 2005). By 2010, 57 percent of Latinos lived in the suburbs and constituted 18 percent of the suburban population (Guzman et al. 2010). In suburban Cook County, the Latino population grew by 46.5 percent from 2000 to 2010 (Sledge 2011).

Chicago's Latino population is characterized by its youthfulness, U.S. birth, and citizenship status. According to the Pew Hispanic Center (2010), the median age among Chicago Latinos is twenty-eight, but there are marked age differences by nativity: the foreign-born median age is thirty-nine, while the U.S.-born median age is sixteen. A whopping 82 percent of Latinos aged twenty-nine or under are U.S.-born, and 93 percent of Latinos aged seventeen and under are U.S.-born. Around 58 percent of the CMA Latino population is U.S.-born, and 73 percent of Latinos in the CMA are citizens. Among the foreign-born, 60 percent are adults, two-thirds arrived in the United States after 1990, and 31 percent are naturalized U.S. citizens. There are roughly equal numbers of male and female Latinos in the CMA, although men slightly outnumber women aged twenty-five to thirty-nine. The magnitude of Latinos' youthfulness and growing numbers is best captured in school enrollment figures. In the CMA, Latinos make up 29 percent of the student population (Guzman et al. 2010). In the Chicago Public Schools, Latinos constitute 45 percent of the student population. In the suburban CMA, Latino enrollment increased 60 percent over the past decade, bringing the Latino student population up to 23 percent (Guzman et al. 2010). Additionally, the two local four-year public universities are Hispanic-Serving Institutions.

Chicago's importance in Latino historiography does not lie solely in its relevance as a traditional Latino immigrant gateway, or the sheer numbers of Latinos, or the youthfulness of its population, but rather on the historical diversity of the Latino population in the city and the intra-Latino dynamics that fostered the early development of Latino panethnicity. Unlike other U.S. regions where single Latino populations predominated until the past two decades, major Latino groups have had a historical presence in Chicago since the 1940s with the establishment of Mexican and Puerto Rican communities and a smaller but significant Cuban presence by 1970 (Fernandez 2012; Innis-Jiménez 2013; F. Padilla 1985). Since the 1980s, increasing numbers of Guatemalans, Ecuadorians, and a sprinkling of other Latino groups have made Chicago their home. In 2010, the Latino population in the CMA was overwhelmingly Mexican (84 percent) but had a significant Puerto Rican population (10 percent) and smaller numbers of Guatemalan, Ecuadorian, Colombian, and other Latino groups (Brown and Lopez 2013).

Despite national diversity among Latinos in Chicago, these groups share a similar context of reception marked by their racialization as "other" in a racially divided city. Fernandez (2012) argues that the Mexican and Puerto Rican experiences in Chicago have much in common. Both groups became pawns in the racial stratification that characterizes the city: from residential segregation to employment discrimination. Upon arrival in Chicago, these groups concentrated in different parts of the city, but these early communities were not isolated from each other as racial discrimination often brought Mexicans, Puerto Ricans, and Cubans together at the few Catholic churches, restaurants, and dance halls that welcomed them and on factory floors (E. Padilla 1947; F. Padilla 1985). Today, Latino groups continue to concentrate in particular areas of the city; however, in these areas, Latinos of different national origins increasingly live and work side by side and attend the same schools and churches. The increasing diversification of the Latino population means that Latino millennials are more likely to interact with members of other Latino groups more often and in diverse contexts.

The cohabitation of multiple Latino groups for the past six decades has had a profound effect on intra-Latino dynamics in Chicago (see Aparicio 2016; DeGenova and Ramos-Zayas 2003; Fernandez 2012; E. Padilla 1947; F. Padilla 1985; Pallares and Flores-González 2010; Pérez 2003; Rúa 2001). Indeed, the presence of diverse Latino groups with common struggles of displacement and discrimination led to early expressions of Latino panethnicity in Chicago. In a pioneering study of Puerto Ricans and Mexicans Elena Padilla (1947), documented a growing panethnic sentiment—in spite of some tension—among Mexican and Puerto Ricans in the 1940s. Despite early manifestations of Latinidad—a shared sense of identity—she incorrectly predicted that Puerto Ricans would become absorbed by the Mexican population. Forty years later, Felix Padilla argued in his seminal work *Latino Ethnic Consciousness* (1985) that a panethnic political awareness among Mexican and Puerto Rican activists, which he labeled "Latinismo," had developed in Chicago. Fueled by shared experiences of discrimination, and deploying a discourse of cultural similarity, Mexicans and Puerto Ricans rallied together to fight for their educational, political, and economic rights (F. Padilla 1985). Felix Padilla argued that although the basis of commonality for Puerto Ricans and Mexicans lay in their assumed cultural similarity, the driving force for Latinismo was a common fate as marginalized and maligned that led to temporary political coalitions between these groups.

Studying the interaction between Mexicans and Puerto Ricans in Chicago, DeGenova and Ramos-Zayas (2003) argue that the "unequal politics of citizenship"—signified by Puerto Ricans' undeniable status as U.S. citizens and Mexicans' questionable legal status—stand in the way of long-lasting panethnic unity. Other scholars acknowledge the role of citizenship in Chicago's Latino intradynamics but downplay its salience, arguing that Latinidad is not necessarily fraught with contention over the issue of citizenship (Aparicio 2016, 2016; Flores-González and Rodríguez-Muníz 2014; Garcia and Rúa 2007; Pérez 2003; Rodríguez-Muñíz 2010; Rúa 2001). Pérez (2003) found that Puerto Rican and Mexican women in Chicago hold strong opinions about each other: while Mexican women view Puerto Rican women as *rencorosas* (spiteful), Puerto Rican women view Mexican women as *sufridas* (long-suffering women). Despite holding these opinions, Puerto Rican and Mexican women got along and often had very close relationships with each other through community, work, or familial ties. In a study of ethnic festivals in Chicago, Garcia and Rúa (2007) noticed the deployment of both national and panethnic identities at ethnic festivals that, although fraught with some tension, did not lead to intergroup rivalry but rather to tolerance, providing spaces for their concurrent expression and coexistence. Also, research on the 2006 immigrant marches in Chicago show that by construing racialized experiences as "similar, but not identical," Puerto Ricans were moved to join this "Mexican" political struggle (Rodríguez-Muñíz 2010; Flores-González and Rodríguez-Muñíz 2014). In a study of Mexican and Puerto Rican student interaction in a Chicago high school, Rosa (2014, 37) found what Rivera-Servera (2012) calls *frictive intimacy*, or the development of "intimate knowledge of both Mexicanness and Puerto Ricanness . . . often reflected in the invocation of various stereotypes about one another's physical appearance, musical tastes, styles of dress, and language use." He also found that despite recognizing these differences and asserting their own national identities, these youths identified panethnically and found a common ground. This historical context of panethnic identity formation informs Chicago Latino millennials' notions on identity and belonging.

Latino Millennials

To fully grasp why the young participants in my study see themselves as citizens but not Americans, I utilize the concept of "generations" as an analytical lens. A generational approach to the study of Latino racialization may include "generation since immigration," "generations over time," "generation as an age-group," and/or "generation as a historical cohort." Studies on "generation since immigration" compare the first, second, third, and subsequent generations, or they lump these groups into the foreign-born (first-generation) and the native-born (second- or later-generation) populations. For example, Wendy Roth, in *Race Migrations: Latinos and the Cultural Transformation of Race* (2012), compares changing notions of race among Puerto Rican and Dominican immigrants and nonimmigrants "back home." Julie Dowling's *Mexican Americans and the Race Question* (2014) examines racial identification among immigrant and U.S.-born Mexican-origin adults in three Texas locations. And Tomás Jiménez's *Replenished Ethnicity: Mexican Americans, Immigration, and Identity* (2010) studies integration among "later-generation" or "third and subsequent generation" Mexican Americans who trace their family settlement in the United States to prior to 1940.

Other studies take on a "generations over time" approach that focuses on different familial generations—that is, differences between grandparents, parents, and children within the same family. For example, Jessica Vasquez's *Mexican Americans across Generations: Immigrant Families, Racial Realities* (2011) examines racial identity formation in three generations within the same families. In their groundbreaking book *Generations of Exclusion: Mexican Americans, Assimilation, and Race* (2008), Edward Telles and Vilma Ortiz utilize a two-dimensional lens by focusing on "generation since immigration" and "generation over time" in their analysis of intergenerational integration among Mexican Americans in Los Angeles and San Antonio.

The "generation as an age-group" lens examines Latino racialization and integration by dividing the population into different age-groups, such as "seventeen and under" and "eighteen or over," or focusing on a particular age-group. Most notable among these works is Alejandro Portes and Ruben Rumbaut's book *Legacies: The Story of the Immigrant Second Generation* (2001), which focuses on different measures of acculturation (such as educational attainment, language, racial identification, and mobility) among second-generation youths in Miami and San Diego.

Finally, research on Latino "social generations" or "cohorts" focuses on Latinos who were born, and came of age, during a particular historical time and thus share a common social, economic, and political context. Carlos Munoz's groundbreaking book *Youth, Identity, Power:*

The Chicano Movement (2007) details the historic struggles of Chicano youths during the civil rights era. More recently, *Brokered Boundaries: Immigrant Identity in Anti-immigrant Times* (2010), by Douglas Massey and Magaly Sanchez, examines how current political, social, and economic conditions shape identity among first- and second-generation Latinos. Differently from these studies, I use "generation" as a multidimensional analytical lens to examine how a historical moment shapes how those in a particular "social generation" (Latino millennials), "generational age-group" (fourteen- to thirty-year-olds at the time of the study), and "generation since immigration" (U.S.-born second or third generation) experience racialization and understand their place in U.S. society.

Generally, the term "millennials" (or, as they are often called, Generation Y or Generation Next) refers to people born between 1980 and 1995. Millennials are sometimes referred to as the "net" or "digital" generation or as "digital natives" because they are the first generation to grow up with computer technology and to use social media to connect with others (Bennett, Maton, and Kervin 2008; Dungy 2011; Pew Research Center 2014). Dungy (2011) identified this generation's defining moments as September 11, 2001, high school and campus shootings, mobile phones and social networks, YouTube, Wikipedia, the 2008 recession, and the election of Barack Obama as president of the United States. As a group, millennials are by far the most racially diverse and politically liberal generation and generally support same-sex marriage, interracial marriage, and the legalization of marijuana; this generation is also more economically insecure and faces more debt and lower economic prospects than previous generations (Pew Research Center 2014).

Latino millennials share many of the traits that characterize the millennial generation more generally, but racialization processes shape their social, economic, and political experiences in particular ways. We need to take into account these cohort-specific experiences to understand why Latino millennials see their position in U.S. society as marginal. The social, economic, and political moments that mark Latino millennials differ from those of previous cohorts. The Latino baby boomers, born between 1946 and 1964, consisted mostly of Mexicans and Puerto Ricans who grew up during the post–World War II economic boom and came of age in the civil rights era. They were raised by "Mexican American

generation" parents who emphasized assimilation as the road to mobility. Failing to achieve mobility, they became politicized during the civil
rights era and made demands for equality through organizations such
as the American G.I. Forum, the Brown Berets, and the Young Lords.

Born between 1965 and 1980, the Latino Generation X reaped the
gains from the expanding educational and economic opportunities that
resulted from civil rights legislation and affirmative action programs.
This generation also witnessed an increase in immigration from Central
America, South America, and the Caribbean that diversified Latino communities, and the enactment of the Immigration Reform and Control
Act (IRCA) of 1986, which granted permanent residence and set 2.7 million undocumented immigrants on the path to citizenship—the bulk of
whom were Latinos. Despite these gains, Generation Xers were tainted
with notions of juvenile superpredators that cast black and Latino youths
as a new breed of violent and remorseless criminals that led to stricter
zero-tolerance and three-strike laws, lengthier sentences, trial of minors
as adults, and increasing rates of incarceration for minority youths.

As a result of increased Central and South American migration starting in the 1980s, Latino millennials—born roughly between 1980 and
1995—are the most diverse Latino generational cohort. Reflecting this
diversity, as well as political and media influences, they grew up with the
terms "Hispanic" and "Latino" in the popular lexicon and in everyday
life. Latino millennials are also a generation whose members have increasingly grown up away from traditional immigrant gateways, in new
immigrant destinations in suburban and rural areas. Although some
of their families benefited from the IRCA, what they remember is the
increasingly restrictive national and local immigration policies and enforcement following the passing of the Illegal Immigration Reform and
Immigrant Responsibility Act (IIRIRA) of 1996, which led to increased
enforcement and securitization at the U.S.-Mexico border, as well as
an increase in raids, detention, and deportations nationwide. They did
not have to live near the border to feel the impact of federal policies, as
state and local enforcement made many communities unwelcoming for
immigrants. Nor did they have to be immigrants themselves to be affected by enforcement and the growing nativist sentiment that targeted
"Latino-looking" people. The terrorist attacks of September 11, 2001,
were another formative moment for many Latino millennials, further

fueling anti-immigrant sentiment and exacerbating restrictive immigration policy and enforcement in the form of the Homeland Security Act of 2002.

Despite a restrictive political environment, Latino millennials also witnessed the unprecedented mobilizations for immigrant rights that swept the nation during the spring of 2006 (see Voss and Bloemraad 2011; Pallares and Flores-González 2010). H.R. 4437—popularly known as the Sensenbrenner Bill—which sought to reclassify undocumented status as a felony and to criminalize anyone who assisted the undocumented, prompted many millennials to engage politically for the first time by joining these protests (Flores-González 2010). These mobilizations also crystallized the meaning of citizenship and its protections and marked many Latino millennials' initiation into politics. While Latino millennials supported the election of Barack Obama to the presidency with hopes that he would deliver comprehensive immigration reform, Obama's presidency stepped up immigration enforcement and carried out unprecedented numbers of deportations, furthering Latino racialization. These social and political events have profoundly shaped how Latino millennials understand their place in U.S. society.

The Study

My interest in this topic stems from a mixture of personal and professional experiences. Despite being a U.S. citizen by birth and being "assimilated" in many dimensions—highly educated, proficient in English, intermarried, middle-class, living in the suburbs—and being a light-skinned Latina who "passes" as white as long as I do not speak or reveal my name, I do not identify as American or as white. This is partly due to being born and raised on "the Island" (Puerto Rico), where "Americans" are clearly defined as (mostly white) people from the mainland. But to a large extent it is also due to my experiences as a Latina in the mainland, where my "otherness" comes out in daily interactions. During almost two decades as a professor and researcher, and despite being a Generation Xer, I find that my former Xer and current millennial U.S.-born Latino students also feel at odds claiming an American identity. I also found this feeling among Latino youths who participated in the massive immigrant rights mobilizations that took place in Chicago in 2006 and 2007 (Flores-González 2010). In-depth interviews with sixty U.S.-born Latino youths who participated in these marches showed that their participation was motivated by their and their family's exclusion from the imagined American community (see Flores-González 2010). Many of the youths talked about being "U.S.-born but not American," or being a "different kind of American." Wondering if this sentiment was shared mostly by those who are politically active, or if it is a widespread sentiment among Latinos, I developed a second set of interviews that delved more deeply into issues of identity and belonging among ninety-seven U.S.-born Latino youths, both participants and nonparticipants in the immigrant rights mobilizations. From this second set of interviews emerged a more complex picture of the impact of racialization on Latino subjectivity as citizens but not Americans. Although it is informed by the first set of interviews, this book is based on the second set.

My analysis is based on ninety-seven in-depth interviews with U.S.-born Latino millennials in Chicago conducted from February to May 2009. The criteria for participation were being a U.S.-born citizen of Latin American ancestry and being between the ages of fourteen and thirty. Participants varied in generational status: seventy-four were second-generation, twenty-two were third-generation, and one was fourth-generation. National origin distribution among participants roughly resembles the composition of the Latino population in the Chicago area: Mexican, 70 percent; Puerto Rican, 7 percent; Ecuadorian, 2.6 percent; Guatemalan, 2.6 percent; Colombian, 2.6 percent; Cuban, 1.7 percent; Dominican, 0.8 percent; Peruvian, 0.8 percent; Costa Rican, 0.8 percent; Argentinian, 0.8 percent; Bolivian, 0.8 percent; and the remaining 9 percent of mixed national origin (Mexican white, Mexican Puerto Rican, Mexican Guatemalan, Mexican Cuban, Puerto Rican Brazilian, Mexican Argentinian). Fifty-nine of the youths grew up and live in the city of Chicago, twenty-six grew up in the suburban CMA, six were from satellite cities (Aurora, Joliet, Peoria), and five grew up out of state (one of the youths did not provide this information). Sixty-one of the youths were college students, thirteen had college degrees and were employed in professional jobs, eighteen youths had not attended college and worked in factories or in technical, sales, or service jobs, and five were high school students. Fifty-two were young women and forty-five were young men. Only four of the youths were members of mixed-status families (at least one parent is undocumented), and the rest had parents who either were citizens by birth or naturalization or had permanent legal residency.

The study subjects were recruited by referral and snowball sampling in which undergraduate research assistants used their social networks to identify potential participants. This strategy resulted in the recruitment of Latino youths living in different contexts within the CMA—ranging from Latino city neighborhoods to white suburban communities. Expanding recruitment from the city to the near suburbs yielded participants from a single Latino national origin as well as youths from interethnic, interracial, and mixed-status families. The interviews, which were conducted in English, ranged in length from forty to ninety minutes. All participants were assigned pseudonyms, and in some instances a few details about their lives that are not relevant to the analysis were altered to ensure confidentiality. All interviews were transcribed and initially coded by the undergraduate research assistants to identify general themes. I conducted four additional rounds of coding, with the initial round focused on identifying general themes, the second round on breaking down these themes into subthemes, a third round to further analyze these subthemes, and a fourth round that focused on each thematic category as a whole. In addition, a research assistant recoded the interviews, checking for consistency and accuracy. The interview guide was divided into five main areas: demographics, identity, family history, transnational links, and political socialization and participation, with particular questions on participants' views on, engagement with, and participation in immigration-related issues. In this book, I focus mainly on the identity section, which includes questions on self-identification and the meaning given to ethnicity, race, citizenship, and Americanness, and the impact that everyday racializing experiences have on identity. Although I concentrate on the identity section, the data presented and the analysis also draw from other sections of the interviews.

Organization of the Book

In this introductory chapter, I have presented the three themes that marked these youths' sense of alienation from political and social membership in the American imagined community, situated my study within the broader theoretical frameworks on race and belonging, and provided methodological and analytical details of this project. In the rest of the book, I delve deeper into why and how the Latino millennials whose stories are portrayed here understand themselves as citizens but not Americans.

Chapter 2 provides a detailed account of these youths' encounters with everyday racism. I frame this chapter as the racial politics of race and space in order to examine how the physical and cultural characteristics that make Latino millennials visible also mark them as racial, cultural, and national others. This othering in turn casts doubts on their right to belong in particular places and spaces marked as white and erodes their feelings of belonging.

Chapter 3 examines the complexities of ethnic and racial identification among Latino millennials. In this chapter, I provide a critique of the conceptual split of ethnicity and race in sociological theory by arguing that these concepts fail to capture how Latino millennials think about their social categorization. I posit that Linda Martin Alcoff's (2009) call to think of Latinos as an ethnoracial group provides a more suitable framework for understanding the social positioning of Latinos in a society in which race is a primary means of social categorization, and where not having a suitable racial category makes Latinos invisible and marginal, contributing to the feeling that they are citizens but not Americans.

In chapter 4, I put to the test popular assumptions about the U.S. racial structure as a binary characterized by a sharp color line dividing whites on top from blacks at the bottom, or as a triracial structure with a single intermediate "catchall" racial middle. Latino millennials conceptualize themselves as one of multiple intermediate racial categories occupied by Asians, Latinos, Arab Americans, and American Indians, respectively. They also conceptualize Latinos collectively as a racial middle, but individual location along this racial middle varies according to personal characteristics, most notably skin color and phenotype. Overall, I argue that to continue to subsume Latinos under the white or black side of the color line, or lump them together with other groups in the racial middle, glosses over these youths' particular experiences of racialization and contributes to their sense of racial exclusion and marginalization from the American imagined community.

In chapter 5, I examine how Latino millennials conceptualize the political and social aspects of belonging to the American imagined community. Despite being citizens by birth, these youths do not meet the ethnoracial markers associated with Americanness and thus face exclusion in their everyday lives. Elaborating on the cultural citizenship framework, I argue that these youths engage in what I call ethnoracial citizenship by deploying familiar American tropes to challenge their exclusion and demand to be seen and treated as "Americans."

Finally, chapter 6 brings together these three themes—Latinos as an ethnorace, Latinos as a racial middle, and Latinos as "real" Americans—to provide a theoretical alternative to current discourses on race and belonging. Bringing race front and center, I utilize the case of Latino millennials to show how particular events shape the ways in which members of this population makes sense of their place in U.S. society.

2

Latinos and the Racial Politics of Place and Space

The narratives of Latino millennials illustrate the geography of racial politics in everyday life—or how places and spaces are racially marked. The bulk of these youths' racial experiences happen in "white" places and spaces where they are made to feel unwelcome and where their presence is questioned. When asked about his experiences of racism, Raúl, a twenty-one-year-old second-generation Mexican, put it this way: "Very direct racism, which might have been physical or any other form, I wouldn't say that I have [an] exact recollection of that. But I would say that I have felt instances in which I was treated differently for the way that I looked. I guess even the pronunciation of my own name. . . . I think that immediately distinguishes you in a bad way and you cause sort of a social disruption." Raúl's narrative points to the indirect and subtle racism that characterizes the post–civil rights era. By stating that his very presence causes "social disruption," Raúl implies that his transgression into white places and spaces is unsettling for whites. He goes on to illustrate this further:

If a white person is going to a cultural event, they might see it as a hobby, or something exotic for them to see and experience, and not really value it. Almost just like an exhibit at a museum. Whereas if it was the opposite, me going to a predominantly white people social event or cultural event, I think immediately I would be made sure to feel out of place or that I didn't [belong] there. Where in a sense, they expect the exact opposite. They often like to say that some events are exclusionist, and that's only when they don't like to [feel] excluded or not wanted. But when the opposite happens, when a colored person tries to go to a [white] social event or cultural event, I think they're immediately told, or [they sense] that they don't [belong] there because of the lack of interactions they might have within that cultural event.

Raúl denounces the double standard whereby whites often feel entitled to occupy any place and space regardless of its racial marking while non-whites often are unwelcomed in white places and spaces. He likens whites to anthropologists and colonialists because they want "to study and subject my culture and objectify it for their own means, and then, they have the power to define it and misconstrue it as they liked." Raúl points to the unequal politics of race that gives whites license to intrude and appropriate any place and space. He also implies that exclusion is viewed as a problem only when whites feel uncomfortable in social situations—yet the constant exclusion of nonwhites is unproblematic for whites.

Raul's feeling of being a trespasser in white places and spaces is commonplace among Latino millennials. Most of the stories covered in this chapter attest to the geography of racial politics that imbues places and spaces with racial meaning. Contesting the popular rhetoric of color blindness, the narratives show that there are no race-neutral places and spaces. Like Raul's, these young people's stories expose a racial politics dominated by whites who feel they can move without contestation across settings—including nonwhite ones. Although most instances of discrimination happen when Latino millennials "trespass" into white places and spaces, they also happen in nonwhite settings.

In theory, the racial segregation that characterized the politics of place and race during the Jim Crow era dissipated with the civil rights movement. In reality, public spaces continue to be racially marked. As Lipsitz (2011) argues, places and spaces are racially distinct and sustain racial understandings of who belongs, and even places and spaces that appear to be race neutral are racially marked. Most public spaces and institutions are marked as white, and the presence of nonwhites elicits negative nonverbal, verbal, and physical reactions from whites that are meant to make nonwhite others feel unwelcome or out of bounds (E. Anderson 2015; Feagin and Cobas 2014). My interviews with Latino millennials show that public places and spaces are still constructed in exclusionary ways. As these millennials' narratives illustrate, the bulk of their racial experiences occur in white places and spaces, where they are made to feel like trespassers. I found that the racial politics of place and space are manifested in three overlapping and intertwined ways: the racial politics of visibility, the racial politics of othering, and the racial politics of belonging. Distinctions between these three categories are not always clear-cut—rather, there is a great deal of overlap, and experiences could fit into more than one category. I also found that the frequency and intensity of racial experiences depend on the racial context, as well as on individual characteristics (e.g., skin color, gender, language). In this chapter, I sift through the Latino millennials' racial experiences to show the effect of the racial politics of place and space on these youths' sense of belonging to the imagined American community.

The Racial Politics of Visibility

The racial politics of visibility is prominent in Latino millennials' narratives. By visibility, I mean the physical and linguistic features that made these youths identifiable as Latinos. I found that racial experiences often had the dual effect of rendering these youths invisible and/or hypervisible—and often both simultaneously. Most forms of discrimination make them hypervisible by highlighting their physical or cultural differences, drawing attention to their presence, or making them stand out. Some forms of discrimination make them invisible simply by ignoring or not acknowledging their presence, yet this invisibility turns them into the "elephant in the room" because everyone "sees" them but does not acknowledge their presence. What is damaging about these racial politics of visibility is that these youths are always "on": because most places and spaces are marked as white, Latino millennials, being rendered invisible or hypervisible, consistently stand out from the crowd, are singled out as the other, and are made to feel that they do not belong.

The racial politics of visibility tends to play out in predominantly white spaces where Latinos stand out and is also expressed in physical language such as the stares that Latino millennials encounter when entering white places and spaces that make them hypervisible. Stares often happens in "ultrawhite" settings; these spaces are all or nearly all white, are rarely frequented by nonwhites, and are places where nonwhites are not usually welcomed. Hypervisibility is best exemplified by the cliché of people turning around to stare at a newcomer walking into a restaurant. Mariana, a twenty-three-year-old second-generation Mexican, recalls her first experience being stared at when she and her family went to a restaurant in Wisconsin. She says, "It was like the first day I was there, and there is like one Hispanic in that whole population there. Me and my family went to this restaurant, and everyone in there turned around and stared. And it was crazy! I had never really experienced that before. I had lived in Chicago before that, and it's so diverse here and it was just so weird, and my family and I were 'OK, this is awkward.'" That Mariana is familiar with the diversity of Chicago accentuated her shock at being hypervisible, which led to feeling "awkward," uncomfortable, and unwelcomed.

Stares do not occur only in restaurants; they are also very common in stores, where Latino youths' hypervisibility often makes them feel uncomfortable and constructs them as trespassers. Sandy, a twenty-one-year-old second-generation Bolivian, points to the incessant stares she gets while shopping. She says, "Thankfully, I have not experienced discrimination like straightforward. But there has been, like, the situation where I go to a store, and it's all predominately white, and if I go in there, no one says anything, but you can tell by the way that they stare at you, or like you could tell the awkwardness. Like they might be thinking, 'What is she doing here?,' but I never faced it, like no person has ever said anything racist to me, but just like the atmosphere. Sometimes the way they look at you, or their stares!" For Sandy, this hypervisibility—prompted by unwelcoming stares—makes her feel uneasy and out of place.

Although a single individual may sneak by without causing others to raise an eyebrow, or may be largely ignored and rendered invisible, avoiding stares is more difficult when a young Latino person is accompanied by another Latino. The invisibility of one turns into the hypervisibility of many. Among the millennials, young women were more able to fly under the radar when alone, whereas young men tended to attract more attention. Esther, a twenty-one-year-old second-generation Ecuadorian, explains that people do not stare at her when she is alone but do so "when I'm with people of my same race." Dori, a nineteen-year-old second-generation Mexican, also observes that she is stared at when her father, who is "Mexican-looking," is present. Like Esther's, other youths' narratives show that Latinos may be invisible when they are alone but that they become hypervisible when they are with other Latinos.

Other mundane activities such as taking public transportation also involve the racial politics of visibility. For instance, Teresa, a twenty-one-year-old second generation Mexican Argentinian, notices that when she takes the commuter train—a white racial space—"those who are white will not sit next to me even if there are no seats left in the train." José, a twenty-eight-year-old second-generation Mexican Cuban, makes a similar observation; when in the train, he feels "a lot of tension when it's like people from the 'burbs, white folks. . . . Nobody will sit next to you on the train unless you look like them. They sit with their own kind. So even the train is like a smaller model of society. It's like segregated trains." While there are no verbal interactions, physical language cues Teresa and José into the racial politics of the suburban "white" train and the seeming invisibility—yet glaringly obvious presence—of Latinos in this white public space.

Latino millennials also recounted incidents of invisibility at establishments—such as stores and restaurants—in which they were paid no attention while store workers catered to other customers who were white. Liz, a twenty-six-year-old second-generation Mexican, tells of being ignored while shopping in an upscale store. She says that she has "been attended to last or given little to no attention at some high-end retail stores compared to many of the Caucasian customers. One time at Neiman Marcus I asked for a saleswoman's help, and she completely ignored me and took an older-looking Caucasian woman ahead of me when I know for a fact I was there before." Although age could have been a factor leading to the slight, Liz did not believe that she was ignored in deference to an elderly person but rather in deference to a white person. Indeed, other research, such as that by Feagin and Cobas (2014), shows that clerks often ignore Latino customers because they believe Latinos cannot afford the merchandise.

Latino millennials also told stories about their invisibility at restaurants. Arielle, a twenty-one-year-old second-generation Mexican, vividly recalls an incident that happened during her childhood, which exemplifies the racial politics of visibility:

One time when my family and I were at a restaurant, I was younger [and] we were like a family of five and we got there before the other family. The waitress was an American, [a] white woman, and the other family was white. I am sure we got there first. We were waiting a longer time and this family came after us, and the lady automatically sat them first until my mother told the lady, "Look, you know, we were here first, and you just went and sat these people." She did not answer my mom, she acted like she was busy and she did not hear her.

Adding insult to injury, not only did Arielle's family become invisible, but her mother was blatantly ignored and deemed invisible when she complained to the hostess. Michael, a twenty-seven-year-old third-generation Puerto Rican, recalls his friends' experience at a predominantly white restaurant where their initial invisibility turned into rude service: "Servers wouldn't come to their table. I mean like, blatantly. One of them told me that they ordered a meal, and they ordered the meal because they saw someone else eating it, and they were told that they didn't serve that meal anymore." While there could be nondiscriminatory reasons for the subpar service—such as a busy shift or running out of the menu item—the frequency of these experiences validates these youths' interpretation of the incidents as discrimination.

Similarly, Dolores, a twenty-eight-year-old fourth-generation Mexican, recounts a restaurant incident that left a deep impression. After a long day of sightseeing in San Francisco, her family stumbled into what seemed like a family-friendly restaurant only to be ignored and then treated rudely. As Dolores recalls:

> I don't know if it was the way we were dressed or the fact that we did look Hispanic, because my grandmother was with us, and my dad, my mom and my sisters and all that, but we were treated so badly there. It was obvious that we were the only ones being treated badly. We weren't being attended to. The waiter was just downright rude to us. It felt like, "What have we done? What are we doing?" And we really couldn't think of anything [that we were doing that would lead to this treatment], so I wanna say that it was because we looked different than everybody else in there because everybody else in there was white and blond and very, very Anglo-looking. And it kind of hit our whole family [all] at once.

Being the only nonwhite customers, it was not difficult for Dolores and her family to figure out that they were being singled out—first by being ignored and later by being treated rudely—because they were Latinos and not because they were underdressed. Their invisibility and the ensuing poor service they receive at stores and restaurants convey to youths like Liz, Arielle, Michael, and Dolores that they do not belong in these white places and spaces.

Being ignored—or being deemed invisible—happens in other contexts as well, such as when applying to or interviewing for a job. Mary, a nineteen-year-old third-generation Mexican, recounts her experience at a job interview: "I got there before two other white people did, and the white woman saw me sitting there, but instead of choosing me to come in first, she waited and chose one of the white girls that was supposed to have her interview after mine." Mary could clearly see that this was a racist action even though it was unspoken. Experiences like these also point to the racial politics of othering and the racial politics of belonging, as these youths are made to feel that they are different and do not belong in these white places and spaces.

It is their physical features that usually make Latino millennials visible—and particularly their skin color. This becomes evident in the different experiences reported by light-skinned and darker-skinned Latinos. Light-skinned Latinos experience less frequent and less intense discrimination, at least in public settings. Asked if he had ever experienced discrimination, Dario, a twenty-one-year-old third-generation Mexican, responded, "Can't really say I have because most people wouldn't guess I was Mexican. Because visually I am not open to discrimination. If you saw me on the streets and didn't know I was Mexican, you would just think I was some white guy." Similarly, Dolores—who earlier described her family's racial experience at a restaurant—states, "There's nothing that's been overt, like racial slurs or anything like that. Because I am lighter skin, I don't necessarily attract some of the negative behavior that I think other Latinos do have to go through." Like Dolores, these youths are aware that individual racial experiences vary based on one's skin color. Michael, who earlier recounted his friends' experience with discrimination at a restaurant, says, "I think [that] because of my race, my discrimination was not as great as members of my ethnicity have experienced as a darker race. . . . Because I'm a light-skinned Puerto Rican, I have faced discrimination, but much, much less than a lot of my darker brothers." Light skin, then, diminishes discrimination but does not eliminate it. That discrimination is experienced by light-skinned Latinos who can pass for whites attests to the racialization of Latino ancestry that is independent of skin color. Speech accents, surnames, and other cultural markers often give away their Latin American ancestry, which in turn strips them of their Americanness.

The main cultural feature that makes Latinos visible is speaking Spanish. Although Latino millennials speak unaccented English, switching to Spanish is common for those who are used to speaking Spanish with their older relatives or in private familial and communal spaces. Rosa (2016b) argues that Latinos confront what he calls the *ideology of languagelessness*, which casts them as linguistically incompetent. He explains that Latinos experience "the stigmatization of their linguistic practices, whether English or Spanish, as incorrect, too heavily accented, and/or inappropriate for public space" (2016a, 108). Feagin and Cobas (2014, 46) add that this linguistic stigmatization leads to racial-linguistic aggressions as "attempts to undermine the status of Spanish and of Spanish speakers and to discourage the everyday use and spread of the language." These racial-linguistic aggressions include silencing and ignoring Spanish speakers (Feagin and Cobas 2014). The silencing happens when they are bluntly told to stop speaking Spanish in white places and spaces. Feagin and Cobas (2014) and Urciuoli (1998) argue that whites often try to stop others from speaking Spanish because they feel uncomfortable that they do not understand and assume that they are being spoken about. Cecilia, a twenty-six-year-old second-generation Mexican, recalls times when she has experienced silencing, explaining, "There have been occasions when people have told me, my siblings, and other Spanish-speaking individuals that we could not speak Spanish at school or other public places."

While speaking Spanish can make Latinos hypervisible and lead to censure, it can also make them invisible. Ignoring Spanish speakers is another form of racial-linguistic aggression often experienced by these youths. Danila, a twenty-two-year-old second-generation Mexican noticed that "I get discriminated against just for speaking in Spanish"; she recounts an incident in a store when an initially helpful and friendly salesperson changed her demeanor drastically after hearing Danila speak Spanish on the phone. Danila says, "After I hung up the phone with my mom, the saleslady told me that there was nothing here she could help me with and went to a different customer. She didn't want to help me after she heard me speaking Spanish." Although the salesperson's motivations are unclear, her changed demeanor after hearing

Danila speak Spanish conveyed her intolerance for Spanish speakers and her willingness to dismiss them. As the salesperson walked away from her, Danila turned from visible to invisible. For Danila and the other Latino millennials, their physical and linguistic visibility leads to the imputation of otherness and the questioning of their belonging.

The Racial Politics of Othering

Latino millennial narratives also reflect the racial politics of othering. Lipsitz (2011) notes that whiteness is an unmarked or normative category and that nonwhites are cast as others. Frankenberg (1993, 1994) adds that whiteness and Americanness are unmarked or neutral racial, cultural, and national categories, while nonwhiteness embodies racial, cultural, and national difference or otherness. Particularly fitting to the racial politics of othering is Ngai's (2007) concept of alien citizens, or citizens by birth whose physical and cultural traits mark them as foreigners. Through the processes of othering, physical and cultural features are essentialized and taken as inherent to the group (Omi and Winant 2014). Among Latino millennials, I found that while physical and cultural features made them visible, it was the meanings attached to these features that turned them into racial and national others.

Physical markers lead to the essentialization of Latino millennials and the attribution of certain cultural traits, particularly the assumption that they know and practice Latino culture and speak Spanish. It is often assumed by non-Latinos that because these youths are Latinos, they are fully ethnic and eat, sleep, and breathe their culture. Eric, a twenty-one-year-old third-generation Puerto Rican and Brazilian, says, "Most people assume that because of my ethnicity, that I would only do Puerto Rican or Latino things. . . . People assume that I only want to speak Spanish. That I only want to eat Latino food all the time. That I only want to listen to Latino music or do Latino dancing. The fact is, I enjoy all of these, but I enjoy so many other things outside of this realm. But people only limit me to this realm." As the only Mexican at her job, Kate, a twenty-three-year-old second-generation woman, is assumed to be bilingual and is often asked to take calls from Spanish speakers or assist a Spanish-speaking customer even though she is not fluent in Spanish. She says, "At work, people who know I am Hispanic always assume I speak Spanish and I don't, so when we get callers they are all like, 'Kate, can you take this?' And I can't because I don't speak a lick. It's kinda uncomfortable because if you look a certain way they expect you to speak the language." Eric's and Kate's narratives illustrate what Rosa (2016a) calls the *co-naturalization of race and language* whereby Latinos are associated with Spanish regardless of their ability to speak it.

While racial-linguistic aggressions make Latino millennials visible (as described in the previous section), those same aggressions also make them the "other." These narratives show that whites impute Latinos with a permanent language deficiency—what Feagin and Cobas (2014) call the *questioning or doubting of English proficiency* and Rosa (2016a) refers to as the *stigmatization of linguistic practices*—and assume that they must not speak English or speak it only poorly. These doubts shine through in people's reaction of surprise or disbelief at their "perfect" English skills. Ana, a twenty-two-year-old Guatemalan, explains that "they are impressed [at] how you speak Spanish and English well, or they ask me, 'Excuse me, do you understand English?', assuming that I don't speak English." Just because individuals look Latino, other people tend to assume they do not speak English. Cathy, a twenty-year-old second-generation Mexican, says that she has been "insulted behind my back and ended up telling people that I do speak English and I understand what they're saying." Simple things such as a moment of hesitation may be interpreted as a sign of not being able to speak English. When Juan, a twenty-three-year-old second-generation Cuban, was ready to pay for a purse at a department store, he hesitated when he learned the price was higher than he had expected, only to have the salesperson assume that he did not speak English. He recalls, "When the woman at the register told me the total, I stopped to think if I really wanted to buy it for that amount. Since I didn't say anything right away, the lady looked at me and said 'pesos,' like I didn't speak English so she had to tell me the amount in another currency." As Juan's narrative suggests, the saleswoman not only assumed that Juan did not understand her but scornfully stressed in Spanish a Mexican currency term.

These youths are aware that they are seen as immigrant others. Rosario, a twenty-two-year-old second-generation Mexican, comments on her hypervisibility and othering as an immigrant when she says, "I think that when certain people look at me, they see an immigrant. You know who those certain people are [whites]." She adds that "because of the issue of immigration, everyone sees a Mexican and assumes immigrant." Closely tied to the assumption of Latinos as immigrants is the notion of their "illegality" or their undocumented status. Samantha, a twenty-two-year-old second-generation Mexican–Puerto Rican, adds that "to be a Mexican is like a big deal right now because [there are] so many stereotypes that are put on Mexicans [as] far as illegal immigrant stuff is going on right now." Rosario and Samantha know that others view them as immigrants and therefore as non-Americans despite their birthright citizenship.

The racial politics of immigrant othering is expressed through remarks that range from blatant racist statements to muttered comments. In their milder form, these take the shape of ethnic teasing or joking by white peers. For instance, Danny, a twenty-one-year-old second-generation Mexican, faces frequent teasing from peers. He says, "White Americans, they make fun of Latinos. I have some white friends that make fun of me all the time, saying the stereotypical things like 'No speaking no English.' 'Beaners.' I think they see it more as a joke." For Oscar, a fifteen-year-old second-generation Mexican, "mostly it's just people playing around. The beaner thing. Jokes. Stuff like that." Although these comments may be intended as teasing or joking, Latino youths do not find them funny, not only because they are offensive but also because they highlight Latinos' difference and put them on the spot—making them hypervisible—and remind them that they do not fully belong.

Another expression of immigrant othering that these Latino millennials encounter takes the form of racial epithets, which also make them hypervisible. Racial epithets do not necessarily involve interaction—they can happen openly in the street as Latinos are walking by. For example, Lisa, a twenty-five-year-old second-generation Colombian, experienced verbal and physical aggression from strangers while "walking down the street in my neighborhood. . . . My mom, my sister, and I were walking, and somebody threw a carton of milk into the street and yelled 'spic.' I had no idea what that meant. It wasn't until ten years later when somebody brought up that term and I asked, 'What does that mean?' Then they explained . . . and after that I understood what had happened." Lisa was the only one among the millennials to report a physical threat, in this case having a milk carton thrown at her and her mother and sister. Nevertheless, her story suggests that othering is not restricted to white places and spaces, as this incident happened in Lisa's predominantly Latino neighborhood.

Most racial epithets play on stereotypes based on Latinos' presumed immigration status, marking them as non-Americans and implying that they do not belong. Ramiro, a twenty-seven-year-old third-generation Mexican, says he has experienced discrimination that plays on Latinos' presumed immigrant status: "I got picked on a few times. I had people call me all types of names. Of course, they often referred to me as 'Hey, go cut the grass,' 'Go back to Mexico,' or 'Go cross el Rio Grande.' You know, stuff like that." Fran, a twenty-year-old second-generation Mexican, also encountered racial stereotypes; she says, "When I went to the first immigration rally, I remember there was a bunch of people near, and they would just call us wetbacks and illegals, stuff like that. And they didn't even know me [and] that I was born here." Ramiro's and Fran's stories show that regardless of their legal status, Latinos often are racialized as non-American others and therefore as not belonging to the national community.

The racial politics of immigrant othering spills into the workplace and is particularly prominent for those serving the public. Saúl, a twenty-five-year-old second-generation Mexican, has been the object of racial slurs at work. He says he has been "called a spic while serving someone food at my former job. . . . I have been called Pancho and some disturbing jokes about having jumped fences and having kids in Mexico." Javier, a twenty-four-year-old second-generation Mexican, overheard racist comments from patrons at the local park where he worked in the summers as a teen. He recalls that "every time I was out there, you could hear people yelling 'How typical, a Mexican doing lawn work!' I tried to ignore it. I knew I was working for a good reason, but man it was hard to go back out there every day and face that. . . . You know if anything comes up, a fight, confusion, or misunderstanding, someone is always trying to put you down asking if you're legal, or 'go back to your home.' That's just the typical stuff." The matter-of-fact way in which Javier shares his experiences suggests that these incidents are indeed "just the typical stuff" and part of everyday life, yet their frequency does not make them less hurtful; for Javier, it had been "hard to go back out there every day and face that." Sometimes, Latino millennials are subjected to more aggressive verbal attacks from frustrated and angry customers. For instance, Jacques, a twenty-nine-year-old second-generation Mexican French man, had "an unruly [train] passenger yell racial slurs at me, refusing my services because I was Latino." Another Latino millennial tells of catching a customer who stole some items only to be verbally abused with a plethora of epithets. These confrontations remind these youths that they are hypervisible others who do not belong in these white places and spaces.

In addition to their othering as immigrants, these youths experienced othering as racial minorities. The imputation of racial minority status carries with it the imputation of lower academic achievement, lower occupational attainment, and criminality. These youths indicated that teachers often presumed that Latino students are not smart or capable, particularly compared with their white and Asian peers. Elissa, a nineteen-year-old second-generation Mexican, calls attention to the disparate treatment experienced by Latinos at her school. She says, "Throughout my school experience, the teachers have paid more attention to nonminority students and less attention to us when it comes to teaching us the language and reading skills. We tend to be more behind. The other students, like whites, let's say Asians, tend to be more ahead when it comes to math and reading and more advanced in their classes than we minorities are." For Elissa, the lower performance of Latino vis-à-vis white and Asian students is directly related to teachers' lack of investment in their Latino students. Latino students feel that they are not taken seriously and languish in the lower tracks, while Asian and white students are pushed to excel. Carina, a twenty-two-year-old second-generation Mexican, says that discrimination at school is "not very out in my face like 'You're Mexican, get out!' No, not blatant racism exactly. It was more like, 'Oh, why do you want to go to school? You should take on a trade.' Like that kind of racism . . . like more covert." While Elissa tells of being invisible at school and Carina of being perceived as not being college-bound, both stories convey that Latinos are stigmatized as low academic achievers.

Young men are also singled out as low academic achievers, but what stands out in their school stories is their othering as gang members. Octavio, a twenty-year-old second-generation Mexican, recalls how

teachers held negative views of Latino male students that were generalized to the larger group. This othering as "gangster" leads to hypervisibility, which results in more surveillance and punishment at school
for young men, even when they are not involved in gangs. None of the
young women reported experiencing surveillance and punishment at
school. Ricky, a seventeen-year-old second-generation Mexican, says
that "the security guards [at school] are always following us around, but
not the white dudes. They follow around black dudes too, and us." As
these narratives imply, school staff not only hold stereotypical views of
Latino students but also act based on these stereotypes, unleashing educational disadvantages that have dire consequences for these youths' life
chances. Rios (2011) provides a more detailed account of the school consequences of being labeled a gang member. The narratives of the youths
in my study are not isolated incidents but widespread experiences that
highlight Latinos' visibility as racial and national others and erode their
sense of belonging to the American imagined community. Regardless of
the kind of othering they are subjected to, these experiences highlight
Latino millennials' visibility and their otherness while eating away at
their sense of belonging to the American imagined community.

The Politics of Belonging

The racial politics of belonging becomes palpable during incidents in
which the right to be in a particular place and space is contested. Unlike
the politics of visibility, which highlights physical and cultural differences, and the politics of othering, which attaches meaning to these
differences, the politics of belonging marks Latino millennials as outsiders and questions their right to be present in certain places and spaces.
These challenges happen in public spaces where Latinos' mere presence
is questioned. They also occur in white places and spaces such as col-
leges and workplaces where Latinos are deemed unqualified or not fit to
belong. Behind the politics of belonging is the presumption that these
youths do not have a right to be in these places and spaces.

One manifestation of the racial politics of belonging deals with the
right to be present in public spaces without eliciting suspicion or the
assumption of ulterior and nefarious motives. I have already mentioned
that young women became visible "oddities" in stores where they were

stared at or ignored but usually let be, but young men were treated as criminal others in these same places and were made overtly aware that they do not belong there. Young men were kept under close scrutiny or received unrequested and unneeded attention from salespeople because they were suspected of having criminal intentions. Johnny, a twenty-three-year-old second-generation Mexican, says that "when I go into stores people follow me and my friends around and always assume that we are stealing things." Another young man, Juan, added to his earlier account of being treated rudely by a salesperson, saying, "I constantly feel discriminated against when I go out shopping. I consider myself to be a well-dressed individual and I don't dress urban, but yet when I go into a store with more expensive clothes, I feel I am followed around or questioned more often by sales people asking if I need help or if I'm looking for something." It does not matter that Juan dresses well—clearly to signal his middle-class status and that he has no gang affiliation—in hopes of decreasing the chances of being racially profiled; he still elicits suspicion when shopping because he looks Latino and therefore is read as having criminal intentions and thus no legitimate reason to be there. Juan is not alone, as other young men also elicit suspicion in white spaces by their mere presence.

There are other ways in which the imputation of criminality—and gang membership in particular—impacted young men's access to and their right to be in public spaces. Just the simple act of walking home could provoke questioning and pat-downs at the hands of police who suspected the young men of criminal activity. In an earlier statement, Michael argued that he experiences less discrimination because of his light skin color, but that he still experiences discrimination "by cops. I've been called spic. I've been pulled out of cars. I've been randomly searched." Similarly, Danny, who in his comments quoted earlier downplayed discrimination by peers as teasing, has his share of encounters with the police. He says, "When I was younger . . . I would automatically be associated as a gang banger" and was frequently stopped by the police. Danny attributes his interactions with police to "being associated as a Mexican, walking down the street with baggy pants and a hoody, they're going to say, 'Oh, there goes a gang banger.'" This occurs, he explains, even when he is just "walking home [from school]. I'm not spitting. I'm not urinating. Not doing anything to call attention. Just walking home."

So frequent are these experiences that Diego, a twenty-two-year-old second-generation Mexican, likens this relentless treatment from police to being seen as an "enemy combatant" or "homegrown terrorist." Diego recounts an incident that happened when he was fourteen years old and on his way to the Boys and Girls Club, and the police "pulled over, three squad cars, guns drawn, 'Where's the gun? Where's the gun?' 'We don't have no gun.' That's an example. Getting frisked, getting labeled, racially profiled, getting pulled over. 'Hey Latin King, what gang you belong to?' Why do I have to be a gangster? 'What you got on you?' In my opinion, it's us versus them. That's how I got treated, like an enemy, an enemy combatant. We found a foe or whatever, you know what I'm saying? Like if I'm a homegrown terrorist." That Diego uses the terms "enemy combatant" and "homegrown terrorist" attests to a form of political othering that casts him as dangerous and diminishes his right to be in the streets.

Another iteration of the racial politics of belonging involves these youths' racial exclusion through the discourse of affirmative action. As racial minorities, Latino millennials encountered situations in which their qualifications and merit were questioned. At times, discrimination takes the form of comments made within earshot directed at a generalized Latino "other." Although these comments are usually not directed at a particular person, they are voiced in such a way that Latinos nearby can hear them. This typically involves the presumption of Latinos' lack of academic or professional merit, particularly stigmatizing them as affirmative action beneficiaries, implying that they did not get into college or secure a job based on their own qualifications. Rosalinda, a twenty-year-old third-generation Mexican, vividly recalls overhearing a conversation among white students during a summer orientation at the college she had decided to attend: "I was sitting in the auditorium waiting for the orientation to begin and was overhearing the conversation going on in front of me between a few white boys. They were talking about how blacks and Mexicans only got in to this school because they were black or Mexican. Like we didn't have the right credentials and didn't belong there. And that pisses me off because I got a 29 on my ACT, and had a real good GPA too in high school. I didn't just get in because I'm Mexican, you know." It is unclear if these white students were aware that Rosalinda was within earshot and if she was the intended target of these prejudicial statements, but that does not lessen their impact. Unlike Rosalinda, Orlando, a twenty-two-year-old second-generation Mexican, believes that the racist remarks he often overhears are not directed at him because as a light-skinned Latino, he usually passes as white. Yet he cannot escape "people questioning why I'm in college. Maybe [it's] because of affirmative action, not based on merit or anything like that." While Orlando dismisses most comments as not directed at him, these remarks—along with the more direct questioning he faces—call into question his right to attend college.

Sometimes questioning of Latino millennials' merit is more direct and leaves little doubt that the slight is directed at them. Sofia, a twenty-year-old third-generation Mexican, had such an experience in a college class when she felt that a put-down directed at a generalized other was really intended for her. She says that in class "this girl was talking about how the Mexican people only got in because they were Mexican. And she was like 'My friend got a 30 on her ACT and because she was white she got rejected and how many people were here they had like 17s.' And she was looking at me, and I was like, 'Are you trying to say that I'm not intelligent enough to be here?' She was really out of control. She really made me mad, that was the only time I felt like 'Wow, I'm looked at as a Mexican that doesn't even deserve to be in this university.'" Although this comment appeared to be directed at a "generalized other," Sofia took offense because her classmate cast doubt on Sofia's educational credentials and made her the visible target by looking at her as she spoke.

Leo, a twenty-six-year-old second-generation Mexican, also experienced more direct questioning when he faced doubts from other members of his trade union about his legitimacy to hold and do his job. Leo says that getting a union job is difficult: "So I have heard comments from white guys that I am just there because of affirmative action. . . . I have mixed feelings about it. I don't understand why someone has to know what race you are in order to give you a job. Either someone is qualified or they're not. But, then again, maybe no minorities would have jobs if it wasn't for affirmative action. . . . [It should be taken away] but only under one condition, the employer can't know the race of the applicant until they are hired. That leaves no room for racial discrimination." This frequent wrangling leaves Leo with "mixed feelings" and angry at the need for affirmative action policies to ensure that qualified racial minority applicants, like himself, can have a fair chance at getting hired. Although he feels that affirmative action stigmatizes him, he knows that without it he would not stand a fair chance, regardless of his qualifications. What the incidents related by Rosalinda, Sofia, and Leo have in common is that they make these youths hypervisible, casting them as undeserving "others" (i.e., affirmative action) and making them feel that they do not rightfully belong in these white places and spaces.

Another way in which the politics of belonging plays out is in the association of Latinos with undocumented status, which raises the question of their right to work. Martín, a twenty-year-old third-generation Mexican, says, "When I go look for a job, they ask me if I am a citizen." Teresa, who stated earlier that white people will not sit next to her on the train, also experienced discrimination, explaining, "When I applied to my first job, my boss asked me if my papers were real." Stabs at Latinos' citizenship status are often subtle, as when Yuli, a twenty-three-year-old second-generation Mexican, was taken aback by a coworker's comment about Latinos with undocumented status. Yuli says that "somebody made the comment that if there was ever an immigration raid, that he would be safe and the rest of us would get taken away because we were all wetbacks. Little did he know that I would not get taken away for legal reasons. He, actually, just based on appearance alone, would get taken away. But, yeah, he figured that since we were all working in a factory job that we must all be illegal immigrants." Yuli was upset at the assumption that all Latinos are undocumented, disregarding most Latinos' legality and birthright citizenship.

Some young men's narratives attach being pulled over by the police while driving to their presumed undocumented immigrant status. Manolo, a twenty-two-year-old second-generation Mexican, says, "I have been stopped by police and asked if I speak English as if I was not supposed to know. They treat you like you have just crossed the border here. It's not fair at all." A more intense situation was reported by Manuel, a twenty-seven year old second-generation Mexican. While he was driving across the country with his father, they were stopped by the police and questioned about their citizenship. According to Manuel, the officer was asking him, "'What's your relationship to this man?' This was just last year, this is right after I went to Mexico, coming back. He's like 'Are you a U.S. citizen? Were you born here?' I think that, looking back at it, that it would definitely be a case of like my citizenship was questioned. . . . Asking my dad where are you coming from, you know, like one of those things, they'll split you up and ask us specific questions and then see if they match up. Definitely, my citizenship is involved in that." Stories like Manuel's show that racial profiling is based not only on one's appearance but also on being assumed to be an undocumented immigrant who does not belong. As these narratives reveal, the racial politics of belonging downplays, minimizes, or overtly denies these youths' right to be present, eroding their sense of belonging.

Millennials' Racial Experiences and Their Self-Understandings

The narratives presented in this chapter help us begin to understand why Latino millennials see themselves as citizens but not Americans. Their experiences reveal their dealings with pervasive discrimination in their everyday lives—what other scholars call *racial microaggressions*—that signal their marginality. These racial experiences are typically not blatant but rather conform to the subtle and covert forms of discrimination that characterize the post–civil rights era. These forms of discrimination are more likely to happen in places and spaces that are racially marked as white, and where Latinos stand out because of physical or cultural traits that render them racial or national "others" and define them as outsiders who do not belong.

In this chapter, I have discussed how the racial politics of place and space—which infuses racial meaning into particular settings—and its three interrelated iterations (the politics of visibility, the politics of othering, and the politics of belonging) shape these youths' self-understandings in relation to the imagined American community. Through the politics of visibility, these youths' physical and cultural differences make them stand out in white settings. The politics of othering uses these same physical and cultural differences to mark them as racial and national others, while the politics of belonging uses these physical and cultural differences to construe them as outsiders who do not belong racially or nationally.

As their narratives show, Latino millennials' everyday experience of discrimination vary in frequency and intensity. Because individual characteristics—such as gender and skin color—mediate the type, frequency, and intensity of their racial experiences, not all Latinos are affected equally. Those who are males or who have darker skin tend to experience more frequent and intense racial experiences—and these differences come through in the later chapters. Despite individual characteristics that may tone down negative racial experiences, no Latino is completely immune from discrimination. While discrimination may target different aspects of their sense of self, it inflicts a larger wound when it happens repeatedly and across settings.

Ultimately, these racial experiences convey Latino millennials' marginal status while eroding their sense of belonging to the American imagined community. As Ana succinctly puts it, "Just like because you get discriminated, there [are] not the same rights, and people think that you just don't belong here." The experiences that Latino millennials relate here, along with the experiences presented throughout the book, point to the centrality of race in shaping their self-understandings as marginal members of the American imagined community—as citizens but not Americans.

3

Latinos as an Ethnorace

When asked what term she normally uses to identify herself, how she identifies ethnically, and how she identifies racially, Giselle, a twenty-three-year-old second-generation woman, responded without any hesitation, "Latina," "Mexican American," and "other," respectively. She identifies as Latina because "we've been socialized to be recognized as Hispanic or Latino in the United States." She describes herself as "light-skinned, brown-haired, Hispanic-looking, and by other people I would automatically be seen as either Mexican or Latino." Her ethnic identity as Mexican American is based on "having origins in the country of Mexico" but also on her physical appearance and values. Prodded to explain why she identifies her race as "other," she explains that "the race categories that I know are black, white, Native American, Pacific Islander, or other. And I can't say that I fall within those." To her, to be "other" is "a lack of being recognized." Giselle bemoans her lack of suitable racial choices:

It's forced upon [you] to choose as black or white. But in reality, you really don't identify with such races. And it seems as if this is a somewhat lost population in regard to identity matters. . . . Lost by not having a concrete way to identify such as the African American community will identify as black, or Caucasians would identify as white. Because I know that there are some Latino individuals who identify themselves as white, and there's others who identify themselves as black. And you question that. And it seems like a complex situation for an individual who is of Latin American descent to have, again, like I said, a concrete way to identify.

I begin this chapter by highlighting Giselle's narrative because it illustrates Latino millennials' racial conundrum. Giselle's straightforward answers convey her self-understanding as Mexican and Latina, others' perception of her as Mexican or Latina, and her feelings of perplexity about how any Latino could identify as anything else. Not having a viable racial choice—because Latino is not considered a race, and she does not fit in the white or black category—leaves Giselle feeling dejected and part of an invisible and "lost population" without a "concrete way to identify."

Latino millennials' narratives show that they are required to choose from racial categories that do not fit their experiences or identities, yet they resist attempts to be pigeonholed into conventional racial categories. Unlike other groups with corresponding pairs of ethnicity and race—such as African American/black and Caucasian/white—Latino is not recognized as a racial category for people of Latin American origin. These Latino millennials' narratives bring to light the complexity of categorizing a people who have undergone racialization and as a result see themselves, and are seen by others, as a separate and distinct group but are nevertheless subjected to ill-fitting racial options. In U.S. society, race is the primary means of social categorization, and not having a suitable racial category deems Latinos invisible, casts them as marginal members of society, renders them outside of the imagined community, and contributes to their feeling that they are citizens but not Americans. In this chapter, I examine how Latino millennials construct ethnoracial self-understandings, and what these self-understandings tell us about Latinos'—quite marginal—standing in the American racial landscape.

My analysis shows that Latino millennials' self-understandings challenge our assumptions about race among Latinos. First, I found that these young people do not identify with conventional racial categories and instead largely think of themselves as a racial group composed of people of Latin American ancestry. Second, lacking an appropriate racial term, the majority of these youths borrow from their panethnic repertoire and use "Latino/Hispanic" or a national origin—such as "Mexican"—as racial terms. And while they may not have articulated it directly as a race, all these youths identified panethnically as Latino/as or Hispanics. These panethnic terms have then taken on racial meaning as Latinos increasingly use them as stand-ins for race (see Flores-González 1999; Flores-González, Aranda, and Vaquera 2014). Third, I found that these youths' self-understandings challenge the conceptual splitting of ethnicity and race, suggesting that this familiar framework may not apply to them. Indeed, the stories presented in this chapter, and throughout the book, suggest that the concept of ethnorace may better inform Latino millennials' self-understandings, as well as how others understand Latinos' social categorization. This chapter addresses what Dowling (2014) calls the "question of race" among Latinos and offers a new perspective on Latinos' place in the racial landscape.

Latinos and the Question of Race

For the past four decades, scholars have been debating the "question of race" among Latinos while generally arguing that Latinos are a white subgroup based on their historical classification as whites and their tendency to self-identify as white on the U.S. Census and in surveys. This assumption follows the conceptual split between race and ethnicity that results in Latinos' classification as a panethnic group rather than a racial group. Traditionally, ethnicity and race have been seen as distinct concepts. In simple terms, ethnicity refers to cultural elements—such as language, beliefs, and practices—that distinguish one group from another; in contrast, race generally refers to physically observable differences that distinguish one group from another (Cornell and Hartmann 1998). The U.S. government recognizes five mutually exclusive races: white, black, American Indian or Alaska Native, Asian, and Native Hawaiian or Pacific Islander (U.S. Census Bureau 2011). These racial categories are based on presumed biological, national, cultural, and geographic origin (Morning 2011). Although Latinos come from a particular geographic region in which diverse national origins share cultural similarities, they are not considered a race because they are phenotypically heterogeneous, often racially mixed, and not assumed to share a particular biological or genetic makeup. Because Latinos are typically described as a racially heterogeneous group—composed of people of white, black, indigenous, and even Asian descent—they do not collectively fit into any of the recognized racial categories (Morning 2011; Rodriguez 2000). Instead, Latinos are regarded as a panethnic group composed of people of diverse Latin American national origins (such as Mexican, Puerto Rican, Guatemalan) and varied racial makeup (European, African, Indigenous, and Asian). Given their racial mixture, it is assumed that, as a group, Latinos do not fit into a single racial category, but that individual Latinos may be white, or black, or any of the other races.

Because racial identification (the labels that people use to describe themselves when they have limited choices) is assumed to match racial identity (what people actually believe they are), and racial identity is used as a measure of belonging, some scholars assume that the large number of Latinos who identify as white on the U.S. Census and national surveys confirms Latinos' status as ethnic whites—or at the very least is a sign of their progression toward whiteness and full integration (Tafoya 2004). Latinos' tendency to identify as white on the U.S. Census, their propensity to identify as "unhyphenated Americans," their gains in socioeconomic status (i.e., education, occupation, and income), language attainment, and intermarriage rates, along with decreases in geographic concentration, are taken as a signal of their (impending) assimilation as whites (Lee and Bean 2010; Warren and Twine 1997; Yancey 2003). Other scholars add that differences in ethnic identification among Latinos are reflective of assimilation into different sectors of U.S. society: identifying as American denotes upward or straight-line assimilation, or aspirations toward assimilation into the white middle class; downward assimilation into a minority group is marked by the taking on of racial or panethnic labels; and identification by national origin or as a hyphenated American reflects assimilation into the ethnic group (Portes and Rumbaut 1996, 2001; Portes and Zhou 1993; Zhou 1997).

The notion that most Latinos are white—or becoming white—has been turned on its head in light of significant and long-lasting changes in Latino racial identification patterns. Most notably, Latino identification as white on the U.S. Census dropped drastically from 95 percent in 1970 to 55 percent in 1980—when the "Some Other Race" (SOR) category and multiple racial identifications were introduced. Restructuring of the 1980 census resulted in more than a third of Latinos bypassing the five standard government-sanctioned racial categories (white, black, American Indian or Alaska Native, Asian, and Native Hawaiian or Pacific Islander) and opting for SOR as their racial choice and writing in their national origin or the panethnic terms "Hispanic" or "Latino" (Rodriguez 2000). Despite further changes in the 1990, 2000, and 2010 censuses, 44 percent, 42 percent, and 37 percent, respectively, of Latinos continued to mark SOR. Findings from a census experiment in 2010 show that a combined question format that places "Hispanic/Latino" among the standard racial/origin categories lowers the selection of SOR among Latinos and results in nearly all Latinos marking the Hispanic/Latino category (U.S. Census Bureau 2012).

This four-decade-long trend shows that marking SOR is not a hiccup that will fade away with cosmetic changes such as rewording or reordering the questions. This trend also questions the assumption that racial identification reflects one's "actual" racial identity. As soon as a racial alternative was available in the form of SOR, a significant number of Latinos shifted their racial identification, suggesting that perhaps all along their racial identification was based on choosing the least ill-fitting category. In light of these shifts, we need to rethink Latinos' place in the U.S. racial landscape.

In tackling this enigma, scholars argue that racial identification is not based on biological or genetic makeup but on social dynamics that infuse social groupings with racial meaning. Racial identification is now understood as a more complex process that takes into account physical characteristics such as phenotype and skin color, cultural traits such as language, and other attributes including nativity, education, socioeconomic status, age, generation, national origin, geography, segregation, and discrimination (Campbell and Rogalin 2006; Desmond and Emirbayer 2009, Dowling 2014; Jones-Correa and Leal 1996; Perez and Hirschman 2009; Portes and Rumbaut 1996; Roth 2012; Tafoya 2004; Taylor et al. 2012; Telles and Ortiz 2008).

Some scholars argue that Latino SOR identification is a reflection of Latinos' racialized ethnicity, such that Latino ethnic groups have been racialized or marked by cultural as well as physical characteristics, and subjected to the discrimination and exclusion that characterizes subordinated racial groups (Feagin 2013; Golash-Boza 2006; Grosfoguel 2004; Telles and Ortiz 2008; Vasquez 2010). They pose that when ethnic groups are racialized, cultural and physical traits are generalized to all members of the group—even if they do not possess these traits—and their experiences align with those of subordinated racial groups (Feagin 2013; Golash-Boza 2006; Kibria 2002; Telles and Ortiz 2008; Vasquez 2011). These scholars also argue that the racialization of Latinos' ethnicity is reflected in their inconsistent, nonlinear, and multiprong patterns of assimilation that remain well into the fourth generation and leads to a strong showing in some measures of assimilation but not in others (Gans 1992; Telles and Ortiz 2008; Vasquez 2011). Vasquez (2011) argues that Mexican Americans experience "racialization despite assimilation," as even those who by many measures (e.g., language, socioeconomic status, intermarriage) are assimilated, maintain a Mexican American ethnic identity because they are perceived and treated as Mexican others. While racialized ethnicity adds complexity to the question of race among Latinos, it is still based on the notion that Latinos are a largely white ethnic group held back by their experiences on the road to assimilation.

Rethinking the Racial Landscape

Other scholars argue that Latinos' identification as SOR reflects a larger and more profound problem with the conceptualization of race and ethnicity that lags behind how people actually think of and enact these concepts (Almaguer and Jung 1998; Dowling 2014; Flores-González 1999; Flores-González, Aranda, and Vaquera 2014; Frank, Akresh, and Lu 2010; Gomez 2007; Hitlin, Brown, and Elder 2007; Itzigsohn 2004; Perez and Hirschman 2009; Prewitt 2013; Rodriguez 2000; Roth 2012). Kenneth Prewitt (2013), former director of the U.S. Census Bureau, argues that the significant proportion of Latinos choosing SOR reflects the irrelevance of a racial categorization scheme founded on outdated eighteenth-century color-based notions of race. The continued reliance on pigmentocracy as the basis of race fails to capture the changing meaning of race, which is now about more than biology or phenotype and includes nationality, culture, and geographic origin (Morning 2009; Pascale 2008; Phinney 1996; Rodriguez 2000).

Some scholars conclude that Latinos' identification as SOR—and particularly their use of the term "Hispanic/Latino"—reflects a status more akin to race than to ethnicity (Dowling 2014; Flores-González 1999; Flores-González, Aranda, and Vaquera 2014; Frank, Akresh, and Lu 2010; Hitlin, Brown, and Elder 2007; Itzigsohn 2009; Perez and Hirschman 2009; Roth 2012). Frank, Akresh, and Lu (2010) argue that Latinos' propensity to self-identify as SOR attests to the redrawing of racial boundaries. Rather than expanding to absorb Latinos as part of the white or black races (blurring of racial boundaries), these authors stress, racial boundaries are enclosing Latinos (intensifying racial boundaries) as a separate racial group. Hitlin, Brown, and Elder (2007) stop short of calling Latinos a race, instead advocating for the switch from race to social origin as a more accurate and significant classification scheme. They contend that the conceptual division of race and ethnicity has little resonance among Latinos, as these are socially equivalent concepts. In an analysis of the 2010 census, the Pew Research Center (2015) found that Latinos think of their Hispanic/Latino background as part of their racial identity.

While in previous works I also called for viewing Latinos as a race, a deeper analysis of my data suggests that ethnorace may be a more fitting concept for describing Latino millennials' self-understandings of their place in the U.S. racial landscape. David Hollinger (1995) poses that social categorization in the United States is characterized by an ethnoracial pentagon composed of five groups: Anglo-Americans, African Americans, Asian Americans, Native Americans, and Hispanics/Latinos. The term "ethnorace" was first used by David Theo Goldberg (1997) to describe social groups that are interchangeably defined as ethnic and racial, are simultaneously viewed as both ethnic and racial, or whose classification has wavered from ethnic to racial over time. Elaborating on Goldberg's concept, Linda Martín Alcoff (2009, 122) defines ethnorace as a group "who have both ethnic and racialized characteristics, who are a historical people with customs and conventions developed out of collective agency, but who are also identified and identifiable by bodily morphology that allows for both group affinity as well as group exclusion and denigration." Alcoff argues that Latinos should be thought of as an ethnoracial group and that doing so gets around the flawed division between race and ethnicity. She adds that an ethnoracial categorization clearly sets Latinos' experience apart from that of other ethnic groups deemed assimilable and recasts what appears to be a bumpy assimilation pattern as an expression of their own ethnoracial group. Alcoff believes that, as a concept, ethnorace allows for a more extensive and inclusive definition that incorporates Latinos' ethnic, racial, class, and gender diversity. Silvio Torres-Saillant (2003) adds that ethnorace also accounts for the common exclusion and disempowerment that affect Latinos despite their diverse national, ethnic, or racial backgrounds. In this chapter, I set out to show that the ethnorace framework is a suitable tool for understanding Latino millennials' place in the U.S. racial landscape. While Alcoff offers a philosophical argument about why Latinos are an ethnorace, here I present an empirical application of her argument. Before discussing Latino millennials' fit as an ethnorace, I discuss how these youths identified ethnically and racially, and how their self-understandings begin to elucidate the question of race among Latinos.

Racial and Ethnic Identification among Latino Millennials

Unlike in the U.S. Census and other survey-based research, participants in my study were not given predetermined categories to choose from but instead were asked open-ended questions that allowed them to use any terms they thought best described them. More specifically, they were asked to state their ethnic and racial identification and then answer questions geared to uncover their understandings of, and the meanings they attach to, ethnicity and race. Three main findings stand out from their answers. First, Latino millennials do not identify in conventional racial terms. Only 6 percent used a standard racial term: 3 percent white, 1 percent indigenous, and 2 percent white Hispanic (or Hispanic white). That so few identify using standard racial categories shows that these categories do not fit. Furthermore, the narratives of youths who identified as white reveal what can be called *racial dissonance*, in that their stated racial identification does not match their racial identity. As I discuss at length in an article written with Elizabeth Aranda and Elizabeth Vaquera, these youths are "white but not really white" (see Flores-González, Aranda, and Vaquera 2014). That is, their racial identification as white is beset with inconsistencies because they neither consider themselves white nor are necessarily perceived as white by others. For them, "white" seems the best racial option because it suits their light skin color and phenotype, they have been told that white is the racial designation for Latinos, or they use Latin American racial standards by which they are "white Latinos" or "Latino whites." Their explanations show that their racial identification—what they may put down on paper—does not necessarily align with their racial identity or how they actually think of themselves.

Second, these youths' answers fall squarely in the SOR category, with more than three-quarters of participants selecting ethnic or panethnic terms for race. In the absence of an appropriate racial term, they borrow terms from their panethnic repertoire and apply them as stand-ins for race: 40 percent used the terms "Latino" or "Hispanic," while 38 percent applied a national origin to race. In addition to the SOR answers, about one-tenth of the Latino millennials identified in nonracial/nonethnic terms by indicating their race as human (6 percent), none (2 percent), or other (2 percent). Also, a trickle of Latino millennials identified "multiracially" by stating more than one term for race, such as "Latino and Mexican American." Regardless of which SOR term they use, it is clear that the standard and officially recognized racial categories do not apply to them and that they make do with labels that are significant to them and to others. Unlike those who identified as white, these youths' racial identification (how they identify when asked) and racial identity (how they actually identify) are consistent throughout their narratives.

Third, if we assume that selecting two different terms for ethnicity and race reflects a conceptual split, and if we assume that national origin and panethnic labels are discrete terms, then we can presume that Latino millennials understand ethnicity and race as distinct concepts. Three-quarters of them stated two different—although interrelated—terms for ethnicity and race. Just over a third stated a national origin for ethnicity and a panethnic term for race, while another tenth inverted these by using a panethnic term for ethnicity and a national origin for race. There was more variety in the terms used for race—such as national origin, panethnicity, standard racial category, nonracial and nonethnic terms—and more consistency in ethnic identification, as 78 percent of the youths applied a national origin term for ethnicity. While most youths used two different labels for ethnicity and race, there was a significant number—about a quarter—of the youths who did not differentiate between ethnicity and race and applied the same term to both. Most of these youths used a national origin label for both their ethnic and their racial identification.

These findings contribute to scholarly and popular debate on the question of race among Latinos. Does their nonconformity to standard racial identification mean that they are a separate racial group? Does their fairly equal reliance on national origin and panethnic labels for race mean that these terms are equivalent? Does their tendency to use two different terms for ethnicity and race mean that they subscribe to the conceptual split between race and ethnicity? In general, what do Latino millennials' self-understandings about ethnicity and race tell us about the question of race among Latinos? And, more important, what do their self-understandings tell us about the U.S. racial landscape and Latinos' place in it?

Latinos Millennials in the U.S. Ethnoracial Landscape

My data show that Latino millennials' self-understandings challenge current conceptualizations of Latinos' race and highlight their marginal—and invisible—standing in the American racial landscape. Current definitions of race leave little room for Latinos to maneuver racially, suggesting that Latino millennials' self-understandings—as well as how they are understood by others—may be best explained by an alternative conceptualization. My analysis suggests the ethnoracial framework, as spelled out by Alcoff (2009), as a fitting alternative. In the following sections, I examine how the three main components of this framework are reflected in Latino millennials' narratives. The first element is what I call Latino millennials' *coupling of ethnicity and race* that results in these concepts being interchangeable, deployed simultaneously, and used contextually. The second element speaks to Latino millennials' identification—by others as well as themselves—by bodily morphology or what can be called a *Latino prototype*. The third element points to Latinos millennials' sense of a similar heritage—Latin American ancestry and cultural similarities—that I refer to as the *weight of Latin American ancestry*.

Coupling Ethnicity and Race

The first element of Alcoff's (2009) ethnoracial framework that comes through in the Latino millennials' narratives is the coupling of ethnicity and race, either directly or indirectly. Those who couple ethnicity and race directly view these concepts as equivalent and see little need for using more than one term. In contrast, those who couple ethnicity and race indirectly tend to use different—but interrelated—terms for each. Irrespective of their approach, Latino millennials were likely to employ the terms they designated for ethnicity and for race interchangeably, simultaneously, and contextually. That is, they substituted one for the other, employed them at the same time, or deployed them in different contexts.

Slightly over a quarter of the Latino millennials coupled ethnicity and race by employing the same term for both concepts. Most of these youths identify ethnically and racially by national origin, while only a handful identify panethnically. Their narratives show that they view ethnicity and race as equivalent and thus see no need to use different terms. Ricky, a seventeen-year-old second-generation man who is half Puerto Rican, insists that he is Mexican, an identification that is reflected in his ethnic and racial choices when he says, "I don't see what the difference is. . . . If someone asks me my ethnicity, I say Mexican. If someone asks me my race, I say Mexican. People never ask me that anyways, it's more just like 'What are you?' No one says race or ethnicity or nothing like that. . . . And like I said, I consider myself more Mexican than anything." Quite explicitly, Ricky condemns the conceptual separation between race and ethnicity, indicating, "I don't see . . . the difference." Manolo, a twenty-two-year-old second-generation man who identifies as Mexican, also does not buy into the conceptual division of ethnicity and race. He states, "When someone asks me about both my race and ethnicity, I use the term 'Mexican.' This is who I am. I don't think it is necessary for me to use another term."

That these youths identify ethnically and racially by national origin does not mean that they do not identify panethnically. They may use both national origin and panethnic terms when identifying ethnically and/or racially, and often in tandem. For instance, Sofia, a twenty-year-old third-generation woman, identifies ethnically and racially as Mexican but uses the terms "Mexican" and "Latino" in tandem when she says, "Race and ethnicity, they're kind of tightly mixed together, I would just say that they're the same thing. . . . I guess I would say it's kind of the same thing 'cause . . . being Mexican and being Latino it's the same thing for me." Likewise, Eric, a twenty-one-year-old third-generation Puerto Rican and Brazilian who identifies racially and ethnically as Puerto Rican, interjects "Latino" along with "Puerto Rican" in his narrative: "To me, it is both. Ethnically, I am closest to my Puerto Rican roots. Most of my family in the United States is Puerto Rican, so almost always I identify as Puerto Rican. If I want to get specific, I identify as pan-Latino because of my multiple Latino roots. However, I consider myself ultimately Puerto Rican." Like Sofia, Eric prefers to identify as Puerto Rican but also identifies as Latino because of his dual ancestry.

In addition to using these terms in tandem, Latino millennials tend to use national origin and panethnic labels interchangeably. They often begin by referring to national origin and switch to a panethnic term partway through their narrative. For example, Liz is a twenty-six-year-old second–generation woman who identifies ethnically as Mexican American and racially as Mexican, yet, when asked about what it means to be Mexican, she switches to the term "Latina":

> I would have to say that the most stereotypical are my skin color and just overall the facial features. . . . I would say that I am overall considered Latina by my traits. . . . To be Latina in this country sometimes I hear the comments and get the dirty looks from non-Spanish-speaking people when I do not in fact speak Spanish. To be Latina, too, I feel that I get the best of both worlds. I do speak Spanish and celebrate my customs, but yet again I am American born and raised so I have an assimilation of customs. . . . To be Hispanic in this country means that you are sometimes treated like an outsider who does not have a clue about education, different cultures, and so on.

Although Liz was asked about being Mexican, every time she substituted "Latina" or "Hispanic" for "Mexican," suggesting that for her these two terms are equivalent and interchangeable.

As Rodriguez (2000) has stated, Latino identification is contextual and thus varies depending on who asks the questions, who answers the questions, the format of the question (open vs. closed-ended questions), and the context in which the question is asked. In this study, Latino millennials acknowledged that "who asks the question" shapes their answers. Eric, who earlier said he identifies as Puerto Rican, states, "I am only Puerto Rican when I am with other Latinos." With non-Latinos, Eric is Hispanic/Latino, and his Puerto Rican ethnicity is largely irrelevant. For these youths, panethnic terms are usually given to non-Latinos, while more specific national origin terms are used among Latinos.

Almost three-quarters of the Latino millennials in my study couple ethnicity and race indirectly. While it may seem that they subscribe to the conceptual split between ethnicity and race, they also employ their ethnic and racial designations interchangeably, simultaneously, and contextually. Danny, a twenty-one-year-old second-generation man who identifies ethnically as Mexican and racially as Latino and Mexican, uses a sports analogy to illustrate his understanding of the connection between race and ethnicity: "I would say it's [race and ethnicity] the same thing. Well if you say race, you would say you're Latino race, and ethnicity, is your specific type of Latino . . . because then the type of Latino, is your ethnicity. If you can just imagine any professional sport, like I play basketball. That is the race, and the ethnicity is the certain team you play for. That is the way I think of it. So Latino would be the general sport, and Mexican would be the team you play for, like the Bulls." As Danny implies, ethnicity and race are distinct yet interrelated. In viewing Latino as the National Basketball Association and Mexican as the Bulls, he envisions race as the larger category that contains different ethnicities, each corresponding to a different national origin. Another youth, twenty-eight-year-old second-generation Edwin, who identifies ethnically as Mexican and racially as Hispanic, states that race "mean[s] the same as ethnicity. Mexican and Hispanic have very close meanings and to me they have always been interchangeable." Because these concepts are interwoven, and relevant in their daily lives, many millennials use them interchangeably and often simultaneously.

Youths who couple ethnicity and race indirectly deploy different terms depending on the context. For Blanca, a twenty-four-year-old second-generation woman who identifies ethnically as Mexican and racially as Hispanic, how the "what are you" question is asked shapes her answer. She states, "If I'm asked 'What's your nationality?' I usually say 'Mexican.' If it's not specific [to nationality] then I'm, 'Well, yeah, I'm Hispanic.'" The format of the question also shapes how Dolores, a twenty-eight-year-old fourth-generation Mexican who identifies ethnically and racially as Hispanic, answers questions about race, even when the choices presented are inaccurate. Dolores explains, "When race is discussed, usually we're told that as Hispanics, that unless you're black, you're white, so especially when we check demographic boxes and things like that, so it weird for me to say white 'cause they say Hispanic isn't a race so I guess according to the Census Bureau it would be white but that's, umm, [in those cases] I prefer to identify ethnically and culturally rather than racially."

Like Dolores, these youths were quick to observe that their responses on official forms depend on the options available to them. If they are free to choose, they may use national origin, panethnic terms, or a combination of these as they did in this study. But when the choices are limited, such as in the closed-ended questions on official forms, they often do not find the appropriate category to check. Carina, a twenty-two-year-old second-generation woman who identifies ethnically as Mexican American and racially as "other," conveys the intricate contextual nature of identification among Latinos. Carina explains, "The term that I identify myself with . . . It depends on the situation that I am in. If it's like a form and it gives you the categories, say it says Caucasian, black, and Hispanic/Latina, I pick Hispanic/Latina. If it is between Hispanic/Latina, I go with Latina. But if it gets more in detail I would go Mexican American . . . but if it comes out of my free will I would identify more as a Mexican American." As Carina states, when a Hispanic/Latino category is not among the options, as is often the case on official forms that ask for race, many youths are baffled, and they feel they do not fit into any of the categories.

Being forced to choose from standard categories that exclude Hispanic/Latino as an option is a daunting, and often exasperating, task. Danila, a twenty-two-year-old second-generation woman who identifies ethnically as Mexican and racially as Latina, explains how it feels when she has to choose among ill-fitting racial categories. She says, "It's hard because I don't fall into the white or black category. I mean, I don't look white, but I don't look black either. I have a medium skin complexion, but I would not consider myself white. I think it's unfair as to how we have to be either white or black. I don't fit into either one, so it gets me frustrated." As Danila conveys, current racial options do not work for Latinos. She, like many other Latino millennials, chooses Hispanic/Latino if that option is available. José, a twenty-eight-year-old second-generation man who identifies ethnically as Mexican and Cuban but who struggled to find a suitable racial designation and finally selected, hesitantly, "American?" for race, insists that government forms "should have a check box for Latino and Hispanic." If there is no check box for this option, José says, "I would fill out the 'other' [and write in] Latino/Hispanic." Overall, these youths' narratives attest to the interchangeable, simultaneous, and contextual nature of ethnicity and race for Latino millennials, which renders the separation of ethnicity and race, as well as the separation of national origin and panethnic terms, meaningless.

The Latino Prototype

The second element of the ethnoracial framework involves, in Alcoff's (2009, 122) words, being "identified and identifiable by bodily morphology that allows for both group affinity as well as group exclusion and denigration," or what I simply term the *Latino prototype*. In their narratives, Latino millennials say that there is a Latino prototype or a Latino look that enables them to identify fellow Latinos and also enables others—Latinos and non-Latinos alike—to identify them and their peers as Latinos. They describe the physical traits that are linked to Latinos as tanned skin, black hair, dark eyes, and average height. David, a twenty-four-year-old second-generation man who identifies ethnically as Latino and racially as Mexican, says that Latinos are identifiable because "the color of their skin is brownish [and] usually they are average height." Liz, who was introduced earlier in the chapter, says, "I would have to say that the most stereotypical are the skin color and just overall the facial features. I would say that I am considered Latina by my traits." Body morphology—or Latinos' appearance—is a visible trait that identifies them as Latinos, at least initially.

About 57 percent of the Latino millennials in my study say that they are perceived by others exclusively as Latinos, or, as Martín, a twenty-year-old third-generation man who identifies ethically and racially as Mexican American, bluntly puts it, "They would identify me as Latino or Hispanic." They point to their physical traits as the main reason they are seen as Latinos. Daniel, a twenty-two-year-old second-generation man who identifies ethnically as Costa Rican and racially as American, is convinced that he is seen as Latino "just based on my physical appearance. I think the easiest way to classify me would be to just say, 'Oh, he's obviously of Spanish descent or Hispanic or something of the sort.'" These youths know that people may not be able to tell what "sort" of Latino they are, something that Zulema, a twenty-four-year-old second-generation woman who identifies ethnically as Hispanic and racially as Mexican, alludes to when saying, "I pretty much think that people can tell I'm Mexican, and if they can't, they know that I am of some sort of Hispanic background." Because these youths look unmistakably Latino—that is, they match the Latino prototype—others readily assume that they are "some sort" of Latino, and therefore they are rarely questioned about their race or ethnicity.

More often than not, the "sort" of Latino these millennials are identified as is Mexican. Their narratives show that Mexican is the default national origin category for Latinos in Chicago. That is, others equate Hispanic or Latino with Mexican and use these terms interchangeably regardless of an individual's actual national origin. Consequentially, non-Mexicans are often assumed to be Mexican. Mariann, a twenty-five-year-old second-generation woman who identifies ethnically and racially as Puerto Rican, says, "You might be mistaken for being Mexican." Eric, whose narrative was presented earlier, points out that Latinos are homogenized as Mexicans. Eric feels "that to most Americans, we are all the same. Most recently, people are learning that there is a difference between Mexican and the rest of Latin America, but mostly because of the increasing Mexican population in the United States. However, I feel that when it comes down to it, they view us as all the same. When one thinks of a Latino regardless of what country he is from—Brazil, Panama, or any other Latino country—they all just view us as Mexicans and living by Mexican culture." To Eric, the labeling of all Latinos as Mexican is largely due to Mexicans' disproportionate representation in the Latino population in comparison to other Latino groups. Thomas, a twenty-three-year-old second-generation man who identifies ethnically as Guatemalan and racially as Hispanic, echoes this feeling by stating, "Most people think I'm Mexican or something. Nobody can ever guess my ethnicity. There's just not a lot of Guatemalans out there. I'm really dark for a Guatemalan, but I guess I do look the part. Curious, but most probably assume I'm Mexican or Asian."

Non-Mexican youths who are assumed to be Mexicans react negatively to the mislabeling. This exasperates Mike, a twenty-eight-year-old second-generation man who identifies ethnically as Colombian and racially as Hispanic but who is often mistaken for Mexican. He observes regional differences in the labeling of Latinos. According to him, mislabeling as Mexican happens less often "on the East Coast because people are more knowledgeable in the East Coast. In the Midwest it is white, black and Mexican. On the east coast it is black, white, Haitian, Jamaican, Puerto Rican, Dominican, Guatemalan, Colombian, Salvadoran." While Mike sees the East Coast as more racially diverse, particularly among Latino groups, he considers the Midwest less diverse, resulting in the lack of recognition for non-Mexican Latinos. Consequently, Latinos tend to fall under the Mexican label, particularly among non-Latinos who make little distinction between Latino groups.

The prominence of skin color for racial ascription shows that Latino millennials with darker skin are frequently classified as Mexican while those with lighter skin are assumed to be Puerto Rican or South American. The only Latino national group to which light-skinned millennials are ascribed is Puerto Ricans; otherwise, they are assigned the generic South American label. For instance, Jim, a twenty-four-year-old third-generation man who identifies ethnically as Latino and racially as Mexican, says, "Sometimes people think I am Puerto Rican. Maybe it's because of my haircut. I am also light-skinned, so they don't look at me as Mexican because most true Mexicans are darker than I am." Similarly, Octavio, a twenty-year-old second-generation man who identifies ethnically as Mexican and racially as Hispanic, shares similar experiences by saying, "Sometimes people think I look Puerto Rican. But most of the time people think that I look Mexican."

Having lighter skin also leads to perceptions of South American origin. Nikki, a twenty-two-year-old second-generation woman who identifies ethnically as Mexican American and racially as Mexican, says that she does not "look Mexican, so they always ask are you Spanish from South America. They see some Latino in me, but they never know exactly from where. That's the main question, and then usually people get surprised I speak Spanish." Orlando, a twenty-two-year-old second-generation man who identifies ethnically as Mexican/Chicano/Latino and racially as white, says that "the majority of the people don't think I'm Mexican. They think I'm usually from South America. . . . No one ever thinks I'm Mexican."

Even among Latinos, ascertaining national origin is often difficult, particularly for the so-called other Latinos, or those who are not Mexican or Puerto Rican. As Esther, a twenty-one-year-old second-generation woman who identifies ethnically as Ecuadorian and racially as Hispanic/Latino, says, "Usually Latinos can tell I'm Latino. When they talk to me they know I'm Latino. But they can't specify Ecuadorian, or anything, but if they do they'll say Mexican or Puerto Rican. But, that's pretty much how people identify me." Similarly, Adamaris, a twenty-one-year-old second-generation woman who identifies ethnically as Guatemalan and racially as Latina, says that rarely is she asked,

"What are you?" because people generally assume that she is "Mexican or Puerto Rican. . . . Because they've told me that I look Mexican or Puerto Rican. People assume that I am."

These youths think that Latinos are more adept than non-Latinos at distinguishing between Latino subgroups. These distinctions are based primarily on skin color and secondarily on other contextual markers. While non-Latinos rely mostly on skin color to ascertain someone's race, Latinos take into account phenotype and nonphysical markers to ascribe ethnicity and race. This comes through in the narrative of Christine, an eighteen-year-old second-generation woman who identifies ethnically as Mexican and racially as Hispanic. Christine explains, "When I was younger people thought I was Polish. And then I got older, people would ask. I might tell them to guess, and they'd say like Polish or Puerto Rican, and I'd say 'No, no,' and they'd ask me again and I'd say, 'Mexican.' With other Latinos it's kind of like 'Oh, yeah.' It's like the term 'you've got a cactus on your forehead,' like you know who's Mexican and who is not kind of thing, so you have a cactus on your forehead, you have a trademark of being Mexican." In this narrative, Christine conjures the popular Mexican saying "tiene el nopal en la frente" ("you have a cactus on the forehead") to explain that Latinos can usually tell that she is Mexican because of her facial features, while non-Latinos rely on skin-color and thus mistake her for white or Puerto Rican. Ricky, who earlier stated that he prefers to identify solely as Mexican, references his darker skin color as well as his Mexican peer group as the reasons people assume that he is Mexican despite his being partly Puerto Rican. Ricky explains, "I hang out with Mexicans, I guess I look more Mexican, and I think I am more Mexican. . . . I'm darker and I'm short. . . . Well, at least compared to all the Puerto Ricans I know. My mom is lighter too. I got more of my dad's color. I have a few lighter Mexican friends, but most Mexicans are darker." Edwin, who argued earlier that race and ethnicity are interchangeable, also points to his peer group as the giveaway of his presumed national origin. He believes that people "are surprised when I tell them I'm Mexican. Everyone just assumes I'm Puerto Rican because I hang out with a lot of Puerto Ricans." Adding to a previous statement, Zulema says that people assume she is Mexican because of her looks and "especially because I live around the Pilsen area, so a majority of people that live there are either Mexican or Hispanic in one way or another." While her looks give away her Latin American origin, her Chicago neighborhood ensures she is seen as Mexican.

About 43 percent of the Latino millennials in my study say that while they are seen as Latinos, they are sometimes mistaken as members of other non-Latino ethnoracial groups—mostly as white and Middle Eastern and to a lesser extent as black, Asian, or Native American. These youths describe themselves as being more racially ambiguous, and their narratives attest to the phenotypic diversity among Latinos. Diego, a twenty-two-year-old second-generation man, points to the fallacy of the Latino prototype:

> It's all in the mind. In this day and age, there's not one particular way that a Mexican or Chicano looks. They're not light-skinned. They're not dark-skinned. They're everything in between. There's dark Mexicans. There's light Mexicans. Typically I would say there's like an image if you think about someone Mexican or whatever. But I don't think that's true, that image. Especially now. You have Mexicans with blond hair and blue eyes. You have Mexicans with darker skin. You have Mexicans that look indigenous. It's everything in between. So, it's really up here. Like identifying yourself as that and then being able to break those stereotypes of what a Mexican or Chicano should look like.

As Diego says, "there's like an image if you think about someone Mexican," but he believes "that's not true." Not fitting into the prototype can lead to one's being mistaken for a member of a different ethnoracial group.

Based on their descriptions, those who say that they are sometimes mislabeled as non-Latino do not fit—or only partially fit—the Latino prototype. Only two youths in my study said that they are at times seen as black and attribute this to their skin color and hair texture. Roberto, a twenty-five-year-old second-generation man who identifies ethnically as Puerto Rican and racially as Hispanic, says that although many people recognize him as Hispanic, there are some "people [who] call me black. They call me Arabian." Similarly, Niurka, a twenty-two-year-old second-generation woman who identifies ethnically as Dominican and racially as Hispanic, says, "Some people mistake me for being black because I am darker and my hair is coarse. They see that I'm darker complexioned but not really dark and they see the texture of my hair." Also, only one Latino millennial, Raúl, a twenty-one-year-old second-generation man who identifies ethnically as Mexican and racially as indigenous, reported that sometimes he is perceived as Native American. Raúl says, "I guess it really depends on the person, and the region which they are from. Some people, I guess, because of my skin tone, they would just identify me as Mexican. Other people, I guess, based on their experiences, have thought that I'm a Native American, because of my long hair. . . . I think more because of my physical features and my brown skin, I guess it gives them more of a clear idea of my ethnic background, which they probably would think is something of Hispanic or Latino." Like Niurka, Raúl identifies his phenotype, skin color, and hair as the traits that lead others to see him as Native American. Raúl was the only youth who reported being mistaken for Native American, a fact that may be related to the low number of Native Americans in the Chicago region.

Some youths say that they are sometimes mistaken as Asian because of their ambiguous looks. Elianna, a twenty-year-old second-generation woman who identifies ethnically as Mexican and racially as Hispanic, says, "I think it's because I'm more light-skinned and it becomes kind of ambiguous to what my race is, so there's kinds of questions about that whether I'm Asian, Pacific Islander, whatever." Ana, a twenty-two-year-old second-generation Guatemalan who identifies ethnically and racially as Latina, is often assumed to be Filipina, while Arielle, a twenty-one-year-old second-generation woman who identifies ethnically as Latina/Hispanic and racially as Mexican, reports, "Sometimes they will be like 'Oh, are you Chinese or Filipino?' and I will be like 'Oh, no. I am this actually,' and they'd be like 'Oh, you look like you could be,' you know they list the whole list of other things I could be." Pablo, a sixteen-year-old second-generation high school student who identifies ethnically and racially as Mexican American, says, "They think I am Filipino because of my eyes and stuff, but mostly [people think I am] Mexican." Appearance is not the only reason they are asked if they are Asian. Justin, a twenty-three-year-old second-generation Mexican who identifies ethnically as Mexican and racially as Latino, says that he has been asked if he is Asian not only because of his phenotype but also because he has an Asian-sounding last name as well as a quiet demeanor. Justin explains, "Based on my physical features . . . physiological features, they always get confused if I'm Asian or not especially in high school, since they knew me by my last name. They thought I was from Japan or something because I used to be very shy, very reserved back then, and they thought [my last name] was my first name. So that's why they thought I was Japanese because I would never speak and they thought I had an English speaking problem back then." Justin's racially ambiguous traits, in combination with his quiet demeanor and unusual last name, led some people to assume that he is Japanese.

Most of the Latino millennials who are mislabeled as members of another ethnoracial group are assumed to be white based on their physical features and skin color. I found that there are gender differences in "what sort of white" young men and young women are perceived to be. Those who were labeled "generically" white are slightly more likely to be young women, while those who are perceived to be of Mediterranean ancestry tend to be young men. For instance, Katerina, a nineteen-year-old second-generation woman who identifies ethnically as Ecuadorian and racially as Hispanic, is certain that she "mostly gets mistaken as [white] . . . like I wouldn't get picked out as a Hispanic because my light skin complexion and my hair is light. And I don't have all those dark features that a typical Hispanic would have." Likewise, Samantha, a twenty-two-year-old second-generation woman who identifies ethnically as Mexican and Puerto Rican, says, "Everyone thinks I'm white because I have very light skin and I don't speak Spanish that well. I guess, I don't speak Spanish fluently." While young women cited their looks as the reason they are mistaken as white, young men pointed to contextual factors that contributed to being mistaken as white. Although David argued earlier that Latinos are identifiable by their brownish skin color and short height, he goes on to say that people assume he is white because "I think it is basically the way I look. I have light skin and I dress very preppy. Also I feel like if people see me with my friends or my fiancée, who are all white, they would assume that I am white too." Because David's peer group is white, he believes that others are more likely to dismiss any thoughts of him as a Latino.

Unlike young women who tended to be perceived as "generically" white, young men were more likely viewed as being Italian or Greek. For instance, Ramiro, a twenty-seven-year-old third-generation man who identifies ethnically as Hispanic and racially as Mexican American, says, "Sometimes they [people] think I'm Italian. They'll ask me if I'm either Italian or Hispanic." Likewise, Nick, a nineteen-year-old third-generation man who identifies ethnically as Cuban and racially as Hispanic American, says that "they'd identify me as Mexican or Italian purely based on my looks. . . . I think I look Cuban, but I also look white, I've been told. People often think I'm Italian." Leo, a twenty-six-year-old second-generation man who identifies ethnically as Latino and racially as Mexican, explains why he is often mistaken for Italian or Greek. He states, "Many people think that I am Greek or Italian because of the way I look. I have an olive complexion and green eyes and I guess people associate that with Italians and Greeks. . . . I think I look Mexican, but I can understand why people confuse that sometimes. I don't care. I just make sure to correct them. . . . I want people to know where I came from and what I am. I am proud to be a Latino." Leo understands that his physical traits lead to others' assumption that he is Italian or Greek, but he sets them straight. Although women were less likely to be perceived as having Mediterranean ancestry, a few said they have been. Sofia, who was introduced earlier in the chapter, says that sometimes people think she is Italian. She explains:

> I get a lot of people telling me Italian, um, Mexican, I get a lot of Hispanic, anything, I've gotten so much different stuff, even at work I've gotten like, Mediterranean and, um, most people can tell that I'm Italian and Mexican. . . . Me personally I think I fit the description [laughs]. I look in the mirror and I look Mexican to myself, but people have said I've been other things, but I think I look [Mexican], people talk to me in Spanish when I go into stores, they think I speak Spanish.

Although Sofia may look Italian or Mediterranean to some, she believes that she fits the Latino prototype. That people address her in Spanish while she is shopping confirms her belief that to other Latinos, she looks Latina.

Another gender difference played out in who was perceived to be a Middle Easterner. Generally young men, and not young women, are perceived as Middle Eastern. For instance, Carlos, a twenty-four-year-old third-generation man who identifies ethnically as Mexican Guatemalan and racially as white, says, "If someone looks at me, they would think that I am whatever I look like to them. So people have identified me in the past as Middle Easterner, some European ethnicity, or as just Hispanic. . . . Just sometimes they ask me questions. I just sometimes get asked what ethnicity I am." Jorge, a twenty-three-year-old third-generation man who identifies ethnically as Mexican and racially as Latino, says that he looks both "Mexican and white. A lot of people think [that] to be Mexican you have to be dark, but those people are just ignorant. I am a light-skinned Mexican and I think I look kind of white. I could definitely pass off for a Middle Easterner or Italian." For Jorge, it was his light skin color that led to his being mistaken as Middle Eastern or Italian, since people tend to think of Mexicans as darker.

Although less frequently, some young women say they have been mistaken as Middle Easterners. Sarah, a twenty-one-year-old second-generation woman who identifies ethnically as Hispanic and racially as Mexican, says, "I've been asked if I was Greek, Italian, Syrian, and Middle Eastern in general." Another young Latina, Elissa, a nineteen-year-old second-generation woman who identifies ethnically as Mexican/Hispanic and racially as Mexican, states that "in the past, though, maybe a few people thought I was a Middle Easterner." Given that people tend to associate the Middle East with Islam, it is possible that young Latinas were less likely to be identified as Middle Easterners because they do not display signs that may mark them as Muslim, such as wearing the hijab or head scarf.

Invariably, Latino millennials encountered the question: "What are you?" This question is faced more frequently by those who are not easily classifiable due to ambiguous physical traits, as well as by those whose physical traits may not match their cultural traits. Lisa, a twenty-five-year-old second-generation woman who identifies ethnically as Colombian and racially as none, sheds light on this issue when saying, "People don't know what I am, so [they ask me] all the time. I guess in high school and in college at some point you're asked 'Oh, what nationality are you?', 'Are you mixed?', 'Where did you come from?', 'Do you speak Spanish?' I guess, it always comes into conversation." Similar to Lisa's experiences, others often cannot select a racial label for Blanca, who stated earlier that people often ask her about her nationality. Blanca says that "some people ask me [what I am] because they don't know. Then they'll be like 'Really? Because you don't seem Mexican.' But for the most part all my close friends I've known for a while so it doesn't really come up anymore. . . . A lot of times I think it's because, I don't know, I don't speak Spanish, I don't know why they expect something different. Maybe because I'm pale." Blanca's pale skin color and her inability to speak Spanish lead to this questioning. Recall José, who denounced the lack of a suitable racial designation but who is also not easily identifiable and is often mistaken for Asian Indian or Middle Eastern. Because of his physical appearance, he is often asked about his origin. He says, "If they asked me 'where are you from?,' [I say] 'I'm American.' 'Well, OK. Where is your family from?' is usually the question I get. Usually when Hispanics ask me, or actually Indian, or Middle Eastern, 'cause I guess I look [like them], they think I am [Indian or Middle Eastern]. They'll be like 'Where are you from?' 'Well, I'm from here. I'm from Chicago, I'm American.' And then they'll ask me again, 'Oh, I'm sorry where is your family from?' and that's when I answer them." Jose's narrative conveys the racial ambiguity that marks these youths and that leads to often passing as Mediterranean (Greek or Italian), Middle Eastern, Native American, or Asian.

Knowing that he looks racially ambiguous, José takes the "what are you" questioning in stride. Not so for Priscilla, a twenty-six-year-old who identifies ethnically and racially as Mexican American and who is really irked by these questions. Priscilla explains, "In terms of people commenting on my ethnicity, I tend to have people that are surprised because there is a big perception about what Mexicans should be like. I guess they should look like more ethnic and by that I mean like more indigenous features, a darker complexion, and obviously I am pretty fair-skinned and definitely do not have a lot of indigenous characteristics. If anything I have more of the French or the Spanish characteristics that kind of happened when those people came to Mexico." Priscilla attributes the incessant questioning to her not fitting the Latino prototype because she is "pretty fair-skinned" and does not have "a lot of indigenous characteristics." And while mislabeling is a common experience for Latino millennials, it is short-lived, as people usually figure out quickly that these youths are Latinos. And once their Latin American ancestry is revealed, they are no longer seen as anything but Latino, pointing to the weight of Latin American ancestry.

The Weight of Latin American Ancestry

The third element of the ethnoracial framework stresses the impact that millennials' Latin American ancestry has on how they are perceived racially. Based on their Latin American origin and its accompanying imputation of particular cultural traits, these youths are assumed to be Latinos regardless of how well they fit into the Latino physical and/or cultural prototype. Once they are recognized as Latino because of their physical traits, cultural traits, or ancestry, other racial labels are out of contention. That is, being identified as Latino dismisses any previous assumption that they are white or that they fit any of the standard races. Even those who can physically pass as white are reassigned racially as soon as it becomes apparent that they are Latino. That their ethnoracial standing is ultimately based on ancestry and not solely on their cultural or physical traits points to the weight of Latin American ancestry.

This weight comes through clearly in the narratives of youths who do not meet the Latino prototype—and particularly those who are initially assumed to be white—but are reclassified as Latinos once their ancestry is divulged. Some youths may not look Latino, but cultural traits give them away, especially speaking Spanish. Javier, a twenty-four-year-old second-generation man who identifies ethnically as Mexican and racially as Latino, says that people assume he is white until he speaks Spanish:

> Well, when I first meet someone, they think I'm white because I'm very light. But, when they hear me speak Spanish, then they ask me what I am. . . . Well, most of the time, if people don't know who I am, they think that I'm white. That can sometimes bother me because I don't want my family to think that I am denying that I'm Mexican, but I can't walk up to everyone I see and say, "Hi my name is Javier, and I'm Mexican!" you know? . . . Well, I mean, they know that people think I'm white. When we all go out together, you can tell people look at us differently.

Javier is aware that he might look white, but when he speaks Spanish, people stop seeing him as white. Often he chooses to "pass" because for him, it is just not worth the effort to correct every person who mistakes him as white.

While these Latino millennials may pass initially as white, once their Latin American ancestry is revealed, the way people see them and interact with them changes. Laura, a twenty-year-old second-generation woman who identifies ethnically and racially as Mexican, says that people generally assume that she is white but quickly realign their racial ascription once they find out that she is Mexican.

> I'm white, as you see, and the part I'm from we are very light, so that's not the typical stereotype of what they think about Mexicans. So when they look at me, they're like, "You're not Mexican." . . . I think sometimes people take you for like the typical stereotype, and for me I think I had a little different experience because I look white. They kind of never categorized me as Mexican at first. So their impressions of me are like, "Oh, you're white, OK." But once they find out I'm a minority, for some reason it kind of changes, and I don't know why but they kind of like feel sorry for me. Like if I say, "Oh, my parents are immigrants," they are like . . . I don't know, it's just like the feeling I get and it's like totally different from when they first approached me, and I don't if it's because they know I'm Mexican now and they're like "Oh!" or it's like shock because I told them I'm Mexican.

When Laura sets people straight by telling them that she is Mexican, she can sense a change. Although she is still the same person, their perception and treatment of her often change.

Sometimes it is the incongruity of physical looks and ethnic markers—such as last names or Spanish language—that triggers a change in categorization. For instance, people often think that Jasmine, a twenty-three-year-old third-generation woman who identifies ethnically as Puerto Rican and racially as human, is white because of her phenotype and her first name. When they find out her last name, they are startled because it is a very common Spanish-sounding last name. Jasmine explains, "People might say I'm Caucasian, or European. They ask me because my last name is obviously Spanish, but they can't figure out why I look the way I do. So I often get asked 'Are you Hispanic?' 'Are you mixed?' A lot of people think I'm mixed." Jasmine notices the change in people's attitudes toward her when they realize that she is Latina. Not being able to reconcile her "white" first name and appearance with a

Spanish last name leads others to assume that she must not be a full-blooded Latina and is instead a half-white Latina. Carina, who earlier pointed to the contextual nature of identification, adds that questions of her racial identity arise when she speaks Spanish. Carina says, "I have been asked just because people don't know what I am. People say that I am either white or Middle Eastern, and once I start speaking Spanish, then they puzzle it together and get that I am Latina or Hispanic." As these narratives illustrative, cultural cues are used by others to realign their perceptions of race among light-skinned Latinos.

Youths who do not fit into the Latino prototype physically or culturally cannot escape ethnic ascription based on their Latin American ancestry. For instance, Dario, a twenty-one-year-old third-generation man who identifies ethnically and racially as Latino, affirms that despite lacking the cultural and physical traits associated with Mexicans, he is still perceived as Mexican by non-Latinos. Dario explains, "If I would have to say, [it would be] someone with a Spanish-speaking background, brownish skin, dark hair. That is what people think I should look like, but obviously you do not need to have those kinds of traits in order to be labeled as a Mexican. . . . I guess I would be like half Mexican or something. I know very little Spanish and do not have brown, but very pale white skin. I guess I'm like an Americanized Mexican." With this narrative, Dario argues that being labeled Mexican has more to do with his Latin American ancestry than with meeting physical and cultural markers. By his own account, Dario is Americanized and points to his lack of Spanish fluency as proof of his tenuous cultural attachment to Mexican culture. Like Dario, it does not matter how marginal other Latino millennials' cultural attachment or appearance is to the Latino ideal; they cannot escape the Latino label because of their Latin American ancestry.

This issue becomes more transparent in the experiences of multiethnic Latinos, particularly those who are half white. These youths are not immune to racialization as Latinos despite their white cultural or physical characteristics, or their half-white heritage. In a study of multiethnic Mexicans who had one white parent, Jiménez (2004) found that most multiethnics identify as Mexican American despite their partial white ethnic background. He attributes their ethnic identification as Mexican American to the weight that skin color, surname, and attachment to Mexican ethnicity have on the ability to "pass" as white. Jiménez found that only those with light skin color and a non-Latino surname can exercise ethnic options, and that among these, Mexican ethnicity is symbolic only for those with a thin attachment to their Mexican heritage. Like Jiménez, I found that Latino millennials who can claim white racial status because one of their parents is white still shy away from whiteness. Sally, a twenty-two-year-old second-generation woman who identifies ethnically as Mexican Albanian and racially as Latina, points to her physical features—and not the fact that one of her parents is white—as the reason "most people assume I'm white. They're surprised that I'm Mexican, probably because of my red hair. They probably think I'm Irish or something!" Although Sally could claim to be white because she has one white parent, she does not identify as white and believes that people initially mistake her for white. Sally's partial Latin American ancestry supersedes her white looks and also her white ancestry.

In a sense, these youths' narratives show that having Latin American ancestry automatically excludes them from being perceived as white even when they do not meet the Latino prototype physically or culturally. Like Jiménez (2010), Telles and Ortiz (2008), and Vasquez (2010), I found that traits that denote white assimilation, such as physical (light skin), cultural (Spanish language), and personal (middle class) characteristics, do not blur the boundaries that separate Latinos as a distinct social group. Because only two youths said they look black—and none identified racially as black—I cannot ascertain if Latin American ancestry has the same weight among dark-skinned Latinos. However, comparative data from Florida with a larger sample of dark-skinned Latinos suggest that Latin American ancestry may also supersede others' classification of dark-skinned Latinos as blacks (Flores-González, Aranda, and Vaquera 2014).

Ethnorace: Merging Ethnicity and Race

The narratives presented in this chapter illustrate Latino millennials' reluctance to choose from ill-fitting conventional racial categories that do not reflect their reality. Lacking a meaningful racial label solidifies their status as marginal and invisible racial subjects. Their racial experiences, as well as how others perceive and treat them, lead them to reject the standard racial categories and to think of themselves as a separate ethnoracial group made up of people of Latin American origin. In the absence of a suitable racial term, these youths select panethnic labels that are meaningful to them and that are recognized by others as representative of people of Latin American origin. In using national origin and panethnic labels—often interchangeably, simultaneously, and contextually—these youths defy the division of ethnicity and race by blurring their conceptual boundaries. In doing so, Latino millennials challenge current racial framing that keeps them as marginal—and practically invisible—players in the American racial landscape.

These youths' self-understandings, as well as how they are understood by others, are best captured by Alcoff's (2009) ethnoracial framework. First, they couple ethnicity and race as equivalent concepts that can be used separately, simultaneously, and/or interchangeably. Second, they emphasize the role of body morphology in defining a Latino prototype as most people share an idea of what a Latino should look like. Third, these youths highlight the weight of Latin American ancestry in their identification, particularly when they lack the physical traits that give away their Latino status. Finally, these youths believe they are part of a distinct ethnorace. When they reject ill-fitting and inaccurate racial labels in favor of more meaningful and representative labels, these youths make themselves visible and relevant, and claim their rightful place in the U.S. racial landscape.

4

Latinos as a Racial Middle

Esther is a twenty-one-year-old second-generation Ecuadorian whose narrative reflects how Latino millennials think of the U.S. racial hierarchy and their place in it. Along with most millennials, she believes that the racial hierarchy is characterized by a color line that places whites on one side and blacks on the other side, and that Latinos occupy an intermediate location—between whites and blacks. When asked, "In the U.S., we tend to think of race in terms of a black and white dichotomy. Where do you and people like you fall within this dichotomy?" Esther responded, "I don't think that we fall on either side. Probably somewhere in between, because, well sometimes physically, people confuse me for white, but I'm not. I don't fit into the white stereotype. And for black, I don't think that I can be grouped with them either. There's a few things from black people and white people that I experience the same as them. I would say that I don't really fall on either side, I fall in the middle."

Like Esther's, other Latino millennials' narratives show that binary notions of the racial structure fail to account for Latinos' racial experiences as nonwhite and nonblack. Although these youths seemingly advocate for a triracial structure with whites at the top, blacks at the bottom, and Latinos occupying an intermediate racial location, their accounts actually reveal a more complex conceptualization of the racial hierarchy and of what has been deemed the "racial middle." In this chapter, I examine how Latino millennials understand the U.S. racial structure, how they conceptualize the "racial middle," and how these conceptions underscore the need for reconfiguring the U.S. racial structure. Being relegated to the white or black side of the color line or lumped together with other groups in the racial middle glosses over these youths' particular experiences of racialization and contributes to their sense of racial exclusion and marginalization from the American imagined community.

These youths' narratives challenge popular notions of the racial structure as a binary marked by a sharp color line that divides whites and blacks and assumes that Latinos, as a racially diverse group, are subsumed under the white or black racial categories depending on their individual (and mostly phenotypic) characteristics. It is assumed that most Latinos fall on the white side of the color line. Objective measures such as Latinos' higher intermarriage rates, lower residential segregation, "white" political views, and racial identification as "white" are taken as signs that Latinos are "like white" or "becoming white" (Lee and Bean 2010; Warren and Twine 1997; Yancey 2003). It is also assumed that while social distance between Latinos and whites is decreasing, an unyielding color line continues to mark blacks as a separate and more disadvantaged racial group (Gans 1999; Sears and Savalei 2006). It is expected that as Latinos, whites, and Asians "gel" together, the white/black binary will change into a nonblack/black binary still characterized by black exclusion (Gans 1999; Lee and Bean 2010; Warren and Twine 1997; Yancey 2003).

Another iteration of the binary racial structure poses that Latinos and Asians, along with blacks, fall on the nonwhite side of the color line. Arguing that Latinos are experiencing social browning, these scholars contend that the boundaries of whiteness are impermeable, and that whiteness will remain elusive for Latinos and Asians (Feagin and Cobas 2014; Takaki 1989). The color line is then characterized by a white/nonwhite binary set to exclude Latinos, Asians, and blacks, relegating them to a racialized status as minorities and preserving the privileged position of whites. The narratives of the youths in this study clearly show that there is a sharp line that separates whites—who are at the top of the racial hierarchy—from other groups, but these youths also drew a line separating blacks, who are at the bottom of the racial hierarchy.

Rather than viewing the racial structure as a nonblack/black or white/nonwhite binary, the young millennials in my study conceptualized the color line as a continuum, with whites at the top, blacks at the bottom, and Latinos (as well as Asians, Native Americans, and Middle Easterners) occupying the space in between. Their assessment resonates with those of scholars who argue for a triracial structure in which Latinos and Asians occupy an intermediate position separate from whites and blacks—or what has been called the "honorary white" or the racial middle (Bonilla-Silva 2004; Frank, Akresh, and Lu 2010; Forman, Goar, and Lewis 2002; Murguia and Forman 2003; Murguia and Saenz 2002; O'Brien 2008; Roth 2012; Tuan 1999). Central to this approach is Bonilla-Silva's (2004) Latin Americanization model, which poses that the boundaries of whiteness and blackness will expand to include light-skinned and dark-skinned Latinos and Asians, respectively, but that the majority of Latinos and Asians will occupy an intermediate racial category he calls the "honorary whites." Bonilla-Silva envisions this tier as a permanent fixture that serves as a buffer between whites and blacks but that lingers closer to the white tier, as honorary whites seek to further distance themselves from blacks and vie for white privilege.

Although these youths clearly see themselves as a racial middle, their conceptualization of the racial middle differs from Bonilla-Silva's single intermediate "catchall" racial tier. Rather, their narratives point to a racial middle composed of multiple intermediate racial categories occupied by Asians, Latinos, Middle Easterners, and Native Americans, respectively. They also challenge Bonilla-Silva's reliance on skin color as the dividing line in his three-tier hierarchy, as their narratives reveal that skin color is part of a larger equation that includes social class, culture, and language—these are the multiple characteristics that mark them collectively as nonwhite and nonblack. These youths' vision resonates with studies pointing to a racial structure in which these groups occupy distinct positions in the racial hierarchy corresponding to the different and unique ways in which each is racialized (e.g., Frank, Akresh, and Lu 2010; Hitlin, Brown, and Elder 2007; Hollinger 1995; Kim 1999; Omi and Winant 2014; Park and Park 1999). Although not specifying what shape it will take, they call for the rearticulation of the racial order to accommodate Latinos. Yet, the racial middle remains largely an undertheorized concept.

Particularly informative for my findings is the racial triangulation model developed by Claire Jean Kim (1999). Kim problematizes the conventional linear and hierarchical biracial and triracial conceptualizations by envisioning the racial order as a plane with two or more axes, each of which reflects one of the multiple dimensions by which groups are simultaneously racialized. Differences in group status, then, reflect that group's location along these axes in relation to other groups. Kim identifies two axes or dimensions: "relative valorization" occurs when the dominant group (i.e., whites) appraises two subordinate groups—such as blacks and Asians—relative to each other; "civic ostracism" refers to the degree to which a subordinate group is constructed as foreign and unassimilable. Asian Americans, she explains, have been valorized as "model minorities" over blacks' "native minority" status but at the same time are ostracized as "foreigners" and "not Americans" while blacks' status as citizens and Americans goes unquestioned. Although Kim's model does not include Latinos, hers is a fitting model for conceptualizing how Latino millennials think of their racial location.

Indeed, the narratives presented in the previous chapters—as well as in this chapter—speak to these youths' dual racialization along these two dimensions: as native minorities (i.e., underachievers, criminals) and as "illegal" immigrants (i.e., foreigners, not Americans). I found that in making sense of their racial middle position, Latino millennials compare their racial experiences with those of other groups. From their narratives, it is evident that these youths see themselves as occupying a slightly superior position than blacks, but a lower position than whites and Asians, on the valorization scale. At the same time, they are lower than these groups on the civic ostracism scale: while Asians and Latinos share the "foreigner" status, it is Latinos who bear the stigma of illegality. Their narratives then point to the existence of multiple racial middles rather than a singular "catchall" racial middle.

The Racial Location of Latinos

In this chapter, I dig deeper into Latino youths' racial understandings to examine their conceptualization of the racial structure and their place in it. I found that their narratives challenge our current notions of the racial structure and the color line. My first central finding shows that these youths' narratives contest the assumption of a binary racial structure. A small fraction (less than a tenth) of the youths tried to fit into the presumed binary racial structure by locating themselves on the white or black side of the color line when they did not identify racially as such. These youths tried to fit into these inadequate options, and most did so reluctantly by choosing "by default" the least incompatible option. Yet, settling for the "lesser of two evils" was not acceptable for a quarter of the Latino millennials who instead simply refused to locate themselves

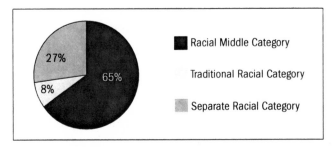

Figure 4.1. Latinos' racial location in relation to whites and blacks

in the racial structure. These youths stated that they were "neither white nor black" but did not offer an alternative vision of the racial structure. In contrast, two-thirds of the Latino millennials did not hesitate to state their racial location as "in the middle" or "in between." These youths clearly pushed for the redefinition of the racial structure by insisting that that there is a racial middle and that they are part of it. Figure 4.1 summarizes how these youths define their position in the racial hierarchy. That so few identified their racial location along the traditional racial categories of white and black challenges prevalent notions of the racial order as a racial binary and the assumption that Latinos, depending on their physical characteristics (i.e., skin color), fall onto one or the other side of the binary. They do not define themselves as white or "like white," and from their experiences they infer that they are not defined by others as white, nor are they privy to the privileges of whiteness. The data also do not support the social browning thesis, as the few millennials who identified their racial position as black do not define themselves racially as black and are not perceived by others as black, despite sharing some experiences of racialization with blacks.

While a few Latino millennials identified their racial location as white or black, the majority of the youths (92 percent) contested the racial binary by rejecting notions of Latinos' whitening or browning. Their narratives convey frustration with a racial structure that does not acknowledge their uniqueness as a group. Some outright rejected the racial binary by refusing to engage with these concepts or else had much difficulty pinpointing where they fit in the racial order. While recognizing that they are neither white nor black, this group could not envision an alternative racial order. Most youths, however, embraced a racial middle position—but this was a racial middle that differs from earlier iterations of the concept.

My second finding shows that these youths' narratives contest the assumption of a "catchall" racial middle. Their narratives offer a more nuanced and complex conceptualization of the racial middle than has been theorized thus far. Those Latino millennials who identified as a racial middle, who constituted 65 percent of the participants, conveyed narratives of difference and insisted on the unique positioning of Latinos in the racial order. While their narratives clearly point to their racial middle status, it is a racial middle that differs from what Bonilla-Silva calls "honorary whites." Rather than being part of a collective racial middle that includes Asians and other groups (as Bonilla-Silva assumes), these young Latinos view themselves as a *separate* racial middle, which suggests that we should think of a racial structure composed of many "racial middles," the positions of which reflect each group's unique racialization.

These youths were not always sure of their precise location in the hierarchy, but they knew that, as a group, Latinos fall somewhere in between whites and blacks. Understanding themselves as lower than whites but not as low as blacks in the U.S. racial structure, these youths located their collective racial position somewhere in the middle of the spectrum, yet their own location in the racial middle wavered depending on individual characteristics and experiences. While most planted themselves solidly in the middle, many identified as a racial middle that tilted toward white or toward black. For these youths, physical traits, cultural and ideological similarities, physical proximity to other groups, social class, and access to privilege and racial experiences interacted to determine their location within the racial middle.

In the following section, I dissect each of the racial locations identified by these millennials—traditional racial categories, "neither" white nor black, and racial middle—to show the inadequacy of our current theorization on racial structure and the racial middle, as well as to begin developing a more complex understanding of the U.S. racial structure.

"By-Default" Traditional Racial Locations

Nine youths located themselves at either end of the racial hierarchy. Although they placed themselves alongside whites or blacks in the racial hierarchy, these youths do not identify with these racial categories. That is, their racial location does not necessarily correspond to their racial identification, as they did not identify racially as white or black, nor do other statements throughout the interview match this racial location. Why did they locate themselves on the white or black side of the color line despite not identifying with these racial categories? The narratives suggest that their racial location choices are their individual attempts to fit into a binary racial order—given their individual phenotypic characteristics—and not reflective of collective, Latino-wide social whitening or social browning processes.

While three of the youths identified their racial location as white, their narratives are seemingly contradictory. That they identify their racial location as white does not mean they identify racially as white, are racialized as white, feel close to whites, or believe they are "like white" or that Latinos, in general, are "becoming white." For them, white is a "default" category, which they reluctantly embrace. For instance, Samantha is a twenty-two-year-old third-generation woman of Puerto Rican and Mexican descent whose racial location as white matches her racial identity as "white phenotypically," as well as how she thinks others perceive her, at least on first impression. Despite being able to "pass" as white, Samantha feels most distant from whites and knows that she is not white. She explains, "I don't really relate to white people except [for] how I look. I don't come from a white background." Placing herself on the white side of the color line had more to do with being a Latina who has "very light skin" and is able to "pass" rather than with being categorically "white."

Another millennial, Araceli, a twenty-seven-year-old second-generation Mexican, assumed that her default location in the racial hierarchy must be white "because we are not from Afro descent." Despite stating that she falls on the white side of the color line, Araceli knows that she is not white. She identifies racially as Mexican, says that people usually assume she is Mexican, feels closer to blacks, and states that the group she feels most distant from are whites. Identifying her racial location as white seems to align with the absence of "black" blood. Not being of "Afro descent" means she is not black, and thus "by default," she must be white in a biracial order.

Sofia, a twenty-year-old third-generation woman with one Mexican and one white parent who identifies racially as Mexican, also says she would have to specify her racial location as white not because of her half-white parentage but because she cannot claim a black location based on her racial experiences. She explains that "personally I would identify like white. If I had to pick, I would be white because I feel closer to that. If you were to identify with black, black people would get mad 'cause you're not black and you didn't go through what they went through." Sofia calls on the notion of "black exceptionalism" by suggesting that blacks' experiences with discrimination are unrivaled, and since her experiences are less severe, she must then fall on the white side of the color line. Samantha, Araceli, and Sofia show in their narratives that choosing white as their racial location is halfhearted at best, not reflective of how they truly feel, and does not mean they are "white," "like white," or "becoming white." Rather, their choice is based on a process of racial elimination whereby lacking more appropriate options, they are by default "white."

For the six millennials who located their racial position on the black side of the color line, this location is also by default. As their narratives show, they neither identify racially as black nor give any indication that Latinos are experiencing social browning as a group. Rather, their racialized experiences as minorities and their exclusion from white privilege draw them to the black side of the color line. For instance, Niurka, a twenty-two-year-old second-generation Dominican who identifies racially as Latina, says her racial location is "black" because "I feel that that is how we are categorized. Anytime you apply for scholarships or anything, we're always grouped together. It's never if you are white, and plus like I feel like we do get the same discrimination." Although Niurka is often perceived as black because of her dark skin, she does not identify racially as black and feels more distant from blacks than from any other racial group. Niurka's contradictory position as not racially black but sharing a racial position with blacks can be understood as an attempt by a dark-skinned Latina to recognize her lack of privilege while also trying to distance herself from what she perceives as a more disadvantaged racial position.

Likewise, other Latino millennials' racial location as blacks had more to do with a shared minority status and racial experiences than with racial identification. This point is more compelling when made by David, a twenty-two-year-old second-generation Mexican who identifies racially as Latino and says that people perceive him as white because he has light skin, yet he stated his racial location as black. David says, "We [Latinos] would fall in the black race just because we are the minority race in most places and still considered inferior to the white race by some whites." Being a minority also played in other millennials' racial location as black. Jacques is a twenty-nine-year-old who identifies racially as Latino and ethnically as Mexican and who, despite having a white parent, places himself on the black side of the color line. He explains, "As far as where I place myself and people like myself within a dichotomy, I guess I'd have to say we fall under black and not white because like I mentioned earlier we are considered a minority." Jacques's narrative shows that Latino ancestry offsets whiteness. For him, having a white parent does not translate into having "white" racial experiences because his Latino side marks him as nonwhite. These kinds of experiences lead Jacques to define his racial position as a minority at the bottom of the racial order along with blacks.

Katerina, a nineteen-year-old second-generation Ecuadorian, is another millennial whose narrative is laden with contradictions. She identifies racially as Hispanic and says she is closer to whites than to blacks "because they [whites] are my friends. Because that is who I hang out with now. It's the people who I grew up with. It's who I have lived with. It's the people that I have been with since pre-K to high school." Nevertheless, Katerina identifies her racial location as black. As she explains, "I would have to fall within the black category because I am a double minority being a woman and being Hispanic." Living among whites may make it clear to Katerina and Jacques that they are not white, highlighting their lack of privilege and leading them to conclude that they must fall on the black side of a racial binary. For these millennials, it is their minority status and their perceived lack of privilege vis-à-vis their white peers, and not necessarily their skin color, that place them at the bottom of the racial hierarchy along with blacks.

That there were only nine youths who identified their racial location on either side of the color line is telling of the unsuitability of a binary racial hierarchy and its limitations in accommodating Latinos. It is also telling that only three of the ninety-seven millennials identified their racial location as white, that these were all women, and that of the five youths who had a white parent, three identified as a racial middle and only one identified her racial location as white, while another identified his racial location as black. Because of the small size of this "by-default" sample, I am unable to develop an analysis of the effect of gender and white parentage on racial location. However, other studies suggest that having a white parent does not necessarily lead to racial identification as white (see Jiménez 2004; Vasquez 2011). That youths who could lay claim to whiteness or blackness because of their parentage, ancestry, or their ability to pass based on physical markers did not place themselves in the white or black category speaks volumes about the inadequacy of the binary order and the inability of the color line to make room for Latinos.

Neither White nor Black

A significant number of Latino millennials stated clearly that they are neither white nor black, but they stopped short of stating they are a racial middle. By choosing "neither," these millennials challenge the prevalent assumption that the racial hierarchy is a white/black binary. A quarter of the participants resisted attempts to be cajoled into a racial binary order where they do not fit, but they also did not offer an alternative. For instance, Marina, a twenty-three-year-old second-generation Mexican who identifies racially as Hispanic, stated "That's the thing, race isn't about black and white. If you're going to define it, don't limit it to just black and white." When asked how she would define it, she simply said, "That is up in the air because I don't know." Ramiro, a twenty-seven-year-old third-generation Mexican who identifies racially as Hispanic, also had difficulty choosing his racial location because he is "Neither. I'm not one or the other. I'm Hispanic." Although, he is Hispanic, Ramiro could not determine where Hispanics fit within the racial hierarchy. Not being able to pinpoint where in the racial hierarchy Latinos fit, Marina and Ramiro believe that Latinos are a separate group and point to their medium-shade skin color as well as distinct racialization as indicators that they fall outside the biracial order. All but one of the youths who identified as "neither" said that people unequivocally assume that they are Latinos. That is, these are not youths who "pass" as white or black. They are unmistakably Latino-looking and thus are perceived by others as Latinos. Many of these youths also recount experiences of discrimination that ensue from being Latino, ranging from subtle to blatant discrimination. These youths also tended to identify racially in panethnic or national origin terms denoting their conceptualization of Latinos as a separate ethnoracial group.

Among those who do not fit into a racial hierarchy is Delia, a nineteen-year-old second-generation Mexican who identifies racially as Latina, and who responded quite energetically when asked about her racial position, "Nowhere. Nowhere. People do look at things like black and white here, but I don't think we fall anywhere around either." When asked if perhaps Mexicans fell somewhere in the middle, she added: "No. Not even in the middle. I think we are completely separate. We just don't [fit]. We're different than blacks and whites. I just don't think we fit."

Javier, a twenty-four-year-old second-generation Mexican who identifies racially as Latino, also rejected the racial middle label. He states, "I guess I don't fit in there at all. I mean some people would say that we are brown, so you would think we are in the middle or even at the black end, but in my opinion, I don't fit on that scale." Martha, a twenty-seven-year-old second-generation woman who identifies racially as Mexican, boldly declares, "I don't believe I fall within the dichotomy just because it is too restrictive because you're either black or white. There is nothing else that you could fall underneath, [that] we can fall underneath. Therefore, I don't believe that the dichotomy is actually existent for people like myself or people who identify as Mexican in the United States." For Lazaro, a twenty-year-old second-generation man who identifies racially as Mexican and who is light-skinned and could pass for white, locating his place on a biracial scale is "kind of complicated." He explains, "If we are speaking specifically in terms of black and white, I could identify as white, but at the same time I am a minority so I can identify myself with blacks as well, but it's kind of complicated to just pick one or the other." Implicit in Lazaro's explanation is his belief that how one is positioned in the racial hierarchy is not simply about physical traits but about how, as a Latino, he is still racialized as a minority despite having "white" physical characteristics.

Some youths pointed to skin color or phenotype as the basis for their not fitting into a binary racial structure. Danila, a twenty-two-year-old second-generation Mexican who identifies racially as Latina, shows her irritation with a racial order that overlooks Latinos with medium skin color when saying, "It's hard because I don't fall into the white or black category. I mean, I don't look white, but I don't look black either. I have a medium skin complexion, but I would not consider myself white. I think it's unfair as to how we have to be either white or black. I don't fit into either one, so it gets me frustrated." While Danila points to medium skin complexion to indicate that she does not fit in the racial order, Irene, a twenty-four-year-old second-generation woman who identifies racially as Hispanic, downplays the role of skin color as a determinant of her place in the racial order "because we tend to use [the term] 'Hispanic' and not the color of our skin."

Forcing Latinos to choose a side of a color line that does not befit them diminishes and glosses over their racial experiences. Sarah, a twenty-one-year-old second-generation woman who identifies racially as Mexican, points to Latinos' increasing visibility when she states, "I think for the longest time people like us have been ignored or neglected. But with the recent influx of Latinos, I think issues regarding us are finally starting to surface. . . . The black/white dichotomy is a whole other issue. I think it'll always be its own separate entity." This point is reiterated by Orlando, a twenty-two-year-old second-generation Mexican who identifies racially as Latino and white. While recognizing that outwardly he may appear white, Orlando feels most distant from whites. In his narrative, he emphasizes the black and white racial discourse that erases Latinos' and Asians' experiences as minorities:

I definitely think [we are] more ignored. It's always black and white. There are now more Latinos than African Americans. Considering that, I do feel like we are ignored. Asians are ignored too. When people come from other countries, they say, "Oh, I never thought of society as black and white until I came to America." I think people in other countries are more open and don't view everything racially like they do here. Generally, I do feel that if you're not white or not black most of the issues are, they don't apply to you pretty much. I feel left out. I can't speak for Asians or other cultures, but I definitely feel as a Latino your perspectives are not really brought up.

Orlando's narrative is representative of these millennials' sense of invisibility and the glossing over of their racialized experiences. Tossing

Asians into the equation strengthens their claim regarding the pre-
ponderance of a white and black racial order that erases other groups'
experiences. Raúl, a twenty-one-year-old second-generation Mexican
who identifies racially as indigenous, takes this issue further when
saying:

> I always remember that whenever it was talked [about] in history books
> at a young age, the African American experience would always be em-
> phasized [from] the slave conditions to the civil rights. You would al-
> ways be taught [about] Martin Luther King and all these other civil rights
> leaders like Rosa Parks and what they did. But then, it would position
> itself as that racism and unjust actions only occurred on the most part
> to African Americans. And in that sense, when a lot of history books
> take that viewpoint or that perspective, I think it leaves out a lot of other
> cultures or races and experiences within this culture, within this coun-
> try, which is completely different in the context in which it happened
> and the ways that it affected them. Considering that it doesn't apply or
> doesn't address the injustices or problems which my race has had within
> this country. So I think [these] issues and historic marginalization and
> injustices are completely obscured and neglected by both Caucasians and
> African Americans.

Without downplaying the discrimination that has profoundly marked
the black experience, Raúl critiques a historical record that "leaves out
a lot of other cultures or races and experiences" in a way that the "historic marginalization and injustices [of other groups] are completely
obscured." Latinos, among other groups, have faced scathing discrimination that relegates them to a lower position in the racial hierarchy and
contributes to their sense of racial invisibility.

Not fitting in is exacerbated by dissimilarities in culture and values
that differentiate Latinos from whites and blacks. Martín, a twenty-
year-old third-generation man who identifies racially as Mexican
American, simply states that he did not feel close to whites "because
we have different cultures and values," while Justin, a twenty-three-
year-old second-generation Mexican who identifies racially as Latino,
provides a more intricate rationale for feeling distant from whites. He
says that Latinos and whites are "like polar opposites. They don't find

that family is the basic unit of life. They're very individualistic and they don't think in the collective good. Because I don't like conflict. I always like to have some harmony established in any circle. So cultures that [are] family oriented like Latin American cultures, those are the ones that I feel keen to because they always think of others instead of themselves." Perceived differences in culture and values that result in not being able to relate or find commonalities with whites also extended to blacks. Jocelyn, a twenty-year-old second-generation Mexican Guatemalan who identifies racially as Hispanic, says she is more distant from blacks because "I'm quiet and most of them are so loud" and jumps to the conclusion that "we don't really click." Stressing cultural differences with the use of stereotypes helps Latinos differentiate themselves from both whites and blacks.

If anything, Latinos' unique racial experiences are closer to the black experience. Adamaris is a twenty-one-year-old second-generation Guatemalan who identifies racially as Latina and recognizes that similarly to "driving while black," there is a "driving while Latino" disadvantage. She explains that she has "been in situations where I've gotten pulled over. Well, not me necessarily, but I've been with people that have been pulled over for no apparent reason, and I think it's because of our being Latinos." Like black youths, Latinos may be typecast as criminals based solely on their appearance and subjected to police stops and other kinds of surveillance (see chapter 2).

Stereotypes like these may make it seem as if Latinos and blacks occupy a common position, but these millennials do not believe they occupy the same racial location as blacks. Dori, a nineteen-year-old second-generation woman who identifies racially as Mexican, explains this point when saying, "I feel like Mexicans fall in the other category, but white people put Mexicans together with blacks because we are of color but we would not put each other in the same group. But to whites we seem the same." Like Dori, these youths are aware that whites indiscriminately lump all nonwhites together but that these groups do not occupy the same place in the racial hierarchy. While acknowledging that he occupies a racial position closer to that of blacks, Raúl calls on negative stereotypes of black criminality and his family's prejudices that prevent him from identifying with that side of the color line. As Raúl states:

I guess the one I would feel a little more close or somewhat close, I guess would be African Americans, because I grew up in an African American community, and I was exposed to their urban realities as well and struggles. But at the same time, I feel a little distant from them as well because of, you know, the negative experience that I or my family had with certain criminals who were African American . . . and also because especially my father, he prohibits [me] from associating with black kids from within my neighborhood. Out of, I guess, his own fear of us becoming street kids as well.

Raúl's statement shows the complex relationship between Latinos and blacks. On the one hand, Latino millennials relate to blacks because of physical proximity or shared experiences of marginalization. But, on the other hand, they (or their parents) use cultural stereotypes to put distance between themselves and blacks, largely to avoid the stigmatization and more disadvantaged position of blacks in the racial order.

While these Latino millennials know that they occupy a different racial location than whites and blacks and that their racial experiences are similar but not the same as blacks', they are reluctant to identify their racial location in a binary order. And while the binary order does not make sense to them, they are unwilling or unable to come up with an alternative racial order in which to place themselves. This reluctance shows not only the inadequacy of the binary racial order to accommodate Latinos but also the sheer dominance of this racial paradigm that blinds them from even imagining an alternative. What distinguishes those in the "neither white not black" category from the "racial middle" category is that while the former cannot pull out of the racial binary, the latter reconstruct the racial binary as a racial continuum where Latinos occupy a separate, intermediate racial location.

Latinos as the Racial Middle

The majority of Latino millennials located themselves in the racial middle. Lacking a precise term to reflect their intermediate or "straddled" status in the racial order, most of these millennials referred to being "in the middle," "in between," and on "middle ground." They also used intermediate color terms like "gray," "tan," "brown," and "both white and black" to denote their in-between location in the racial hierarchy. Along with finding that these Latino millennials challenged notions of a racial binary in favor of a racial middle, I also found that they have a more nuanced and complex conceptualization of the racial middle than our current theorization of it. They do not define the racial middle as a single "catchall" category that Latino and Asians occupy, but rather envision a multitude of racial middles occupied by different groups. Their narratives also show that the racial middle is not a static or uniform intermediate category but instead wavers between whites and blacks. As a group, Latinos may constitute a racial middle, but each person's location within the racial middle varies according to individual characteristics—such as skin color, social class, and racial experiences—that place the person closer to the white or the black side of the color line.

Most Latino millennials position themselves as a solid racial middle, but for some, this racial middle may tilt toward white or black depending on individual characteristics and racial experiences. Figure 4.2 illustrates how these Latino millennials envision the racial order and their place in it. While as a group Latinos are largely "in the middle," some use the terms "gray" and "brown" to signal that despite their group status as a racial middle, their individual location may lean toward either end of the hierarchy depending on their individual characteristics such as phenotype and social class. While "gray" and "brown" are often used as synonyms for the racial middle, for some youths, "gray" seems to denote an intermediate racial location closer to whites. Here the "middle" consists of three subcategories: slightly over half the youths placed themselves squarely in the racial middle, and the two remaining quarters identi-

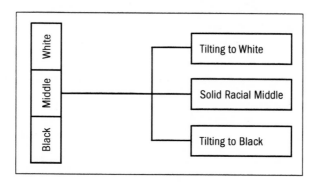

Figure 4.2. Latino racial middle model

fied as a racial middle that tilts, even slightly, toward white or black, respectively.

Even when it tilts toward white, this racial middle differs from Bonilla-Silva's (2004) "honorary whites" tier. These millennials' seemingly closer position to whites in the racial hierarchy was tempered by their greater social distance from whites. Indeed, whites were the group they felt most distant from. Tilting toward white had more to do with their slightly more advantageous position relative to blacks that derived from their individual characteristics that allowed them to "pass," or at the very least to experience less frequent and less intense forms of discrimination (see chapter 2). Locating themselves as a racial middle, these youths emphasize the need to reconfigure the U.S. racial order to account for Latinos' unique racial experiences and intermediate, yet still disadvantaged, position in U.S. society.

The Solid Racial Middle

Slightly over half of these "racial middle" millennials place themselves solidly in the racial middle. They recognize that whites and blacks occupy opposite ends of the color line, that Latinos do not fit into either side, and that Latinos are a racial middle. Janey, a twenty-year-old second-generation woman who identifies racially as Mexican, also locates herself "somewhere in the middle. I don't know. I think somewhere in the middle would be the best just because I don't consider myself white or black." Pointing to her skin, she adds, "I could consider myself white, but I put myself in the middle."

In tune with the color terminology of the U.S. racial order, some millennials used intermediate color terms—such as "brown" or "tan"—to denote this racial middle. Not surprisingly, they used the term "brown" to describe their intermediate racial location, as this term has been used by Chicano and Puerto Rican activists since the 1960s. Mariely, a twenty-three-year-old Puerto Rican who identifies racially as Hispanic and is perceived as Mexican, simply states, "We are in the brown. I don't think it's a black and white dichotomy." Ricky, a seventeen-year-old second-generation man who identifies racially as Mexican, is conflicted and feels that if he had to make a choice in a binary order, he would reluctantly choose black, but he interjects that "brown" is the most appropriate term for him. He explains, "I guess I'd stand on the black side. But I really wouldn't want to stand on either side. I'd probably stand on the line. I don't know. Why do I have to choose a side? Because we don't belong on either side. We're different than blacks or whites. I think we're brown, and I think we should have our own group." Saying that he "stand[s] on the line," Ricky refuses to choose between white and black by claiming a brown racial category. Dolores, a twenty-eight-year-old fourth-generation Mexican who identifies racially as Hispanic and white, explains why brown is the most appropriate descriptor for Latinos:

> It's more of a state of mind and a state of awareness of what your background is that you don't identify [as white or black]. Because when you say white you think of Anglo, you think of gringo. We think of somebody who's not, who doesn't have any type of Hispanic heritage or connection. And that's something we really don't want to identify with. I wouldn't. I think that using brown is helpful to me because it allows you to see something that does not fall into that dichotomy and you're able to see yourself as, not having to choose. Because you couldn't choose between black and white, because you don't fall into either of those. I don't think we fall into either of those.

Dolores finds the term "brown" fitting because the designations of white and black mean not having "any type of Hispanic heritage or connection." Latin American descent, and not their genetic or physical makeup, is the defining characteristic that determines Latino millennials' location as a racial middle.

Similarly, Thomas a twenty-three-year-old Guatemalan who was adopted as an infant and raised by white parents, described his racial position as "right between [white and black]. Brown. It always irks me when census people categorize me as white. I never would consider myself white." Despite not being ethnically Guatemalan and not knowing any Guatemalans while growing up in a predominantly white suburb and with a white middle-class upbringing, Thomas nevertheless identifies ethnically as Guatemalan and racially as Latino because he looks Mexican and his racial experiences lined up with those of Latinos. Implicit in Thomas's statement is the weight of Latin American ancestry on these youths' racial identification and location as brown people regardless of their upbringing (see chapter 3). Similar to the U.S. notion of race based on blood or corporeality, Thomas's Guatemalan blood and Latino looks point to his Latin American ancestry and erase any claim to whiteness despite his white cultural upbringing.

While contextual factors may "whiten" or "blacken" some Latinos, these youths argue that Latinos are still "brown." Danny, a twenty-one-year-old second-generation Mexican who identifies racially as Latino and Mexican, contends that adopting white or black behaviors does not make a Latino white or black. Instead, Latinos remain "brown":

> We're right in the middle. We're our own people because we have our own culture blackanized and Americanized. It's different. You're a product of your own environment. I would think that if a Latino would grow up in a black neighborhood, their traits would most likely be, their character, their dialect, the way they dressed, is going to be influenced heavily by black culture. If you're a Latino growing up in a white neighborhood, you're growing up with Americanized characteristics. You dress that way . . . [but] they would still be in the middle, no matter what. Because they still come from a Latin background. They're just characterized as trying to be white, trying to be black, but overall they would still be in the middle. You're brown! Between white and black, you're brown.

For Danny, no matter how "Americanized" or "blackanized" Latinos may be, or how much they "act white" or "act black," Latinos are neither white nor black but are in their own "brown" group. Like Thomas, Danny implies that anyone with Latin American ancestry is brown regardless of their individual characteristics.

For Mike, a twenty-eight-year-old second-generation Colombian who identifies racially as Hispanic, it was mainly the flexibility engendered by the term "brown" that was more fitting for someone who is "white in the winter and black in the summer." Likewise, Nick, a nineteen-year-old second-generation Cuban Mexican man who identifies racially as Hispanic, used the term "tan" to denote the racial fluidity that characterizes Latinos as a group and that, based on individual characteristics, can place Latinos closer to whites or blacks. Nick explains that "we fall in neither but between the two. This is because if you look at us, we're neither black nor white. We're tan and depending on your color, language, and socioeconomic status you can fall anywhere between blacks and whites, just always between. I would put myself right next to whites, but my dad, for example, who's really dark, would place himself more toward the middle or even nearer to the black category because he has actually been discriminated against and all that." As Nick observes, Latinos occupy an intermediate racial location, but their precise position in relation to whites and blacks is determined by "[skin] color, language, and socioeconomic status," as well as by their racial experiences. That is, Latinos can fall anywhere along the white and black racial continuum.

While the use of the term "brown" was not surprising, the use of the term "gray" by some millennials was unexpected. Some youths referred to the color gray rather than brown to describe Latinos' intermediate position in the racial hierarchy. Some referred to the racial middle as a "gray area," denoting their imprecise location in the racial hierarchy. Among those who said that Latinos fall within a "gray area" was Lisa, a twenty-five-year-old second-generation Colombian who identifies her race and her appearance as Hispanic, and who stresses that "Hispanic culture is a mix of races. So you can't say you're one or the other. You're mixed. You're a combination. [We fall] in that gray area, that in-between that no one acknowledges." Others prefer the term "gray" because it is a more accurate combination of black and white, being a lighter shade than brown and a duller shade of white. For Diana, a nineteen-year-old third-generation Mexican who identifies racially as Hispanic and says she is perceived as Hispanic, the color gray best captures the feeling that Latinos are unrecognized as a group. According to Diana, "[We are g] ray. We are stuck in the middle. A lot of times we get overlooked. That's what it feels like. . . . I think in general we are kind of stuck in the middle. In terms of opportunities, I guess we are more on the black side, because we are not offered the same opportunities as the white side. . . . [We are gray] in the way that we are not as oppressed as the black side but we are not as privileged as the white side." To Diana, "gray" denotes Latinos' fuzzy, undefined, and imprecise location and more accurately conveys a sense of being valued less than whites but higher than blacks.

For others, like Daniel, a twenty-three-year-old second-generation Costa Rican who identifies primarily as Hispanic, identifies racially as American, and is perceived as Puerto Rican, "gray" is simply more compatible with his lighter skin color than the darker shade implied by the term "brown":

> I guess, based on my appearance I fall more within a gray [laughs]. I know that's not really how dichotomies work, but I can't associate myself with being a black person or being a white person. I am not going to be of any other descent than just being Hispanic, and I know that's going to be a hindrance to some people, and the only thing that you're going to have to show for yourself is whether or not your education, or how you have constructed yourself as an individual is worth something. So I guess I am in the middle.

For millennials like Daniel, the term "gray" more closely describes their light skin tone than the term "brown," which they view as closer to black. For instance, Saúl, a twenty-five-year-old second-generation Mexican who identifies racially as Hispanic but says he is perceived by others as white, uses the term "gray" to more accurately denote lighter-skinned "brown" Latinos like himself. According to Saúl, "We are a lighter shade of brown. I could also fall into the gray area. . . . If anything, though, I feel that we are closer to black. . . . People who are brown are considered a minority, and statistically speaking for the most part we have a tendency of being in the bottom of the economic system in the country. . . . I feel that people of brown skin face more oppression. I see a lot of people of brown color marching for rights as black people did throughout the civil rights movement." Saúl understands Latinos as a brown people who, like blacks, face discrimination, yet he uses the term "gray" because it more accurately matches his "lighter shade of brown" skin tone, and others' initial perception of him as white. In addition to more accurately matching their skin color, the term "gray," to these millennials, seems to distance them from both the white and the black experience. Eric, a twenty-one-year-old third-generation Puerto Rican Brazilian who identifies racially as Puerto Rican and is perceived by others as Mexican, considers himself "gray" because he does not relate to the white experience: "I feel that when I try to put myself in their [whites] shoes and look at life and history from their eyes and perspective, I cannot understand the logic in their background. This is not meant as an insult. I just feel that I cannot relate to them at all."

While "color" terms like "brown" or "gray" may give the impression that corporeal characteristics are at the root of these youths' racial middle self-designation, it seems more plausible that they are used simply because they are a logical way to make sense of their location in a color-based racial structure ill-equipped to incorporate Latinos. Indeed, these youths' narratives convey that being a racial middle has more to do with their unique racial experiences and not their skin color or phenotype. Many of the youths who identify as a racial middle measure their racial location not in color hues but relative to non-Latino groups' positions in the racial hierarchy. For instance, Cathy, a twenty-year-old second-generation Mexican who identifies racially as human, is perceived as Latina, and identifies her racial location as "in between," recognizes the racial hierarchy as a spectrum that is marked by a sharp and bold color line that divides whites from everyone else. Cathy's location in the racial middle has to do with being "considered less valuable" than whites. She says, "I think I fall in between the dichotomy because I am considered less valuable to both races. White people are always looking for the next second-class citizen. It started between themselves, the Germans, Italians, Irish, Lithuanians, et cetera, that came to the United States. Then they came together as whites against blacks, then against Asians, then against Latinos, then against Middle Easterners, and currently the last two are at the bottom of the list in white people's eyes." Embedded in Cathy's narrative is Kim's (1999) racial positionality argument, which poses that a group's racial location is relative to other groups and reflects a particular and unique process of racialization along multiple dimensions. Cathy contests the assumption that Latino are becoming white by posing that European immigrants had a different racial experience that allowed them to congeal as whites and stand collectively against nonwhite groups.

That groups are racialized differently and occupy different locations in the racial hierarchy became clear in the youths' narratives about social distance. When asked which groups they felt closer to and most distant from, a clear pattern emerged that signals Latinos' location as a racial middle and that contradicts assumptions about their collective whitening. Quite the opposite picture emerged, as the overwhelming majority of millennials feel closest to other Latinos, closer to blacks, and most distant from Asians and whites. Few mentioned Native Americans and

Middle Easterners, and those who did placed Native Americans as close and Middle Easterners as more distant but not quite as far as whites and Asians. In these youths' narratives, social distance was based on physical proximity, culture, values and ideology, and racial experiences.

Not surprisingly, Latino millennials feel closest to coethnics and other Latinos. They cite physical proximity, cultural and linguistic similarities, shared values, and similar racialization as the reasons they feel closest to fellow Latinos. For example, Danny feels closer to "my own kind . . . Mexican and Latino. . . . The majority of them [Latinos] know what it is like to grow up a Latino. They know what it is like to be discriminated against, have the same family background, exposure to the negative influences to their environment. They understand where I'm coming from." Conversely, he feels most distant from "Europeans. Because I don't really know many of them. I only know a few." Jesús, a twenty-one-year-old Mexican who identifies racially as Latino and says he looks Mexican or Italian, is close to "African Americans. I live by a lot of them. I feel that we all share the same hardships. We can relate to each other." In contrast, he is most distant from "white people. They have it so good. They are treated like royalty here."

Also defying assumptions about Latinos' pull toward whites, the overwhelming majority of youths feel very distant from whites. In fact, whites were singled out as the group that they feel farthest from. These youths identified this distant feeling according to whites' lack of physical proximity, different culture and values, and unequal access to privilege. Growing up in predominantly Latino and African American communities, most youths had little contact or familiarity with whites. Indeed, these millennials' lack of contact with whites reflects structural patterns of segregation. As Diana, a nineteen-year-old third-generation Mexican, says, she is most distant from whites "only because I grew up around a lot of different groups but that was the least that I grew up around." Similarly, Edwin, a twenty-eight-year-old second-generation Mexican states that he is most distant from "probably white people. I don't have a lot of white friends or know a lot of white people. Now that I think about it, all I hang out with are Latinos." Even after getting to know white people, these youths feel distant from whites because their lives seem worlds apart. Elijah, a twenty-two-year-old second-generation Mexican, feels closest to Latinos, close to blacks, and most distant from whites and Asians: "[I feel closer to] probably black. There's solidarity [between Latinos and blacks] and at the same time, there's tension and racism with all three, with white, black, brown, Latinos. With all three, in and out, back and forth. But I think it is definitely, or from my experience, I've found more of a solidarity with black folks, black people." Elijah feels most distance from "white Caucasian, and Indian, Asian. Anything other than black or Latino, Hispanic. Mostly 'cause of culture. . . . It's just rules that each culture has. With white Caucasians, there are things in their culture that I don't know. I can't identify myself with."

Even those who grow up in white suburbia, and who hang out with white peers, feel most alienated from whites. Their physical proximity to whites does not translate into defining themselves racially as whites or necessarily feeling close to whites. Nick, who grew up in the suburbs, feels close to whites but also feels that he has never been completely welcomed in white suburbia. It was not until he moved to Chicago as a young adult that he realized he was not treated equally in the suburbs:

> I feel closer to other Hispanics because a lot of them have to go through the same things that I've had to deal with throughout my life. But I also feel close to whites because I look white. When I moved out of the suburbs to Chicago, I met all new people, and I've been kind of been treated much more equally. I don't know if it's because they don't know I'm Cuban whereas everyone in the suburbs did, or because the city is just more tolerant. . . . I feel more distant from blacks because I just don't have any black friends and I can't relate to their culture, really.

It took moving out of the suburbs for Nick to realize that he was not a racial equal, while in the city he found acceptance. Still his disconnection from blacks is mainly due to his lack of exposure growing up in white suburbia, and later in Latino neighborhoods in the city.

Unlike Nick, many Latino suburbanites grow up with ties to diverse (Latino and African American) neighborhoods in the city. Vallejo (2012) also found that middle-class suburban Latinos have family ties to urban neighborhoods. These youths have relatives, most often grandparents, living in the city, which allows them to spend time there and develop connections to Latinos and to blacks. For instance, Consuelo, a twenty-two-year-old second-generation Mexican who identifies racially as Latina, says, "I think I feel closer to the Caucasian ethnicity only because I grew up closer with them. But I also feel close with African Americans 'cause my grandfather lives in a predominantly black neighborhood, so I was always hanging out with them too." Like Consuelo, youths who grew up in the suburbs were not always isolated from other Latinos or blacks because of their familial ties to Chicago.

Although whites and Asians are at the top of the distance scale, there are differences in how this distance is interpreted. Latino millennials cite lack of physical proximity and vast cultural differences as their reasons for feeling very distant from Asians. Bibiana, a twenty-year-old second-generation Mexican who identifies racially as Hispanic, says that that she does not have any Asian friends, "but it's not because I make sure that I don't. I think it's just because the opportunity hasn't come up that I've met a group of [Asian] people. . . . I have friends from almost every racial group, I just don't have any Asian [friends]." These youths felt more alienated from East Asians than from other Asian youths from India or the Philippines. As Consuelo says, "I'd probably say that the ethnicity I feel less connected to would be the Asian community. I have a couple friends, but I don't know a lot about their culture. [I know] more about the Philippine culture, but not like Chinese or Korean. So I think they're the least I'm connected to." Gonzalo, a twenty-two-year-old second-generation man who identifies racially as Mexican, also feels culturally distant from "anyone from Asia because they have so many different languages and cultures and their letters aren't even the same so you're like 'what does that mean?' You can't really make out the letter 'A' out of a Chinese symbol." Despite their physical and cultural distance from Asians, these Latino millennials recognize Asians as minorities. In contrast, their distance from whites is due to whites' superior position in the racial hierarchy.

What is seemingly a binary model with a sharp color line dividing whites from nonwhites is, rather, a multiracial model with whites at one end, blacks at the other end, and nonwhite/nonblack groups occupying different positions in the nonwhite side of the color line. These youths' narratives add more complexity and texture to our understanding of the racial hierarchy, and of the poorly understood racial middle. While most youths identify themselves as solidly in the middle, others define themselves as a racial middle that tilts toward white or black.

A Racial Middle Tilting toward White

Almost a quarter of these "racial middle" millennials' responses fall in a middle that tilts toward white. Although it would seem that these millennials are in tune with the assumption that Latinos are "becoming white," "like white," or "honorary whites," close examination of their reasoning reveals that tilting toward white is due to "looks," physical proximity, acculturation, social class, and racial experiences. To them, light skin color and/or class position places them closer to whites. This does not mean they see themselves as white but that they are a racial middle that tilts toward the white side of the color line.

"Looks," and particularly skin color, were usually the defining characteristic for millennials who identified as a racial middle tilting toward the white side of the color line. These youths often could pass for whites, at least "visually," but they did not identify as white. Dario, a twenty-one-year-old third-generation man who identifies racially as Mexican but says he is perceived as white and feels closer to whites, explains, "For me, I would say that I fall in the white category, visually. As for Mexicans in general, I think it can go either way. I think that Mexicans experience similar discrimination to blacks, but there are Mexicans like me who are under the radar I guess and blend in with the whites. So I guess I would say they fall right in the middle of the two groups." Yet, "looking white" does not make Dario, or other Latinos, white. Jasmine, a twenty-three-year-old third-generation Puerto Rican who identifies racially as human and says that people usually think she is white, describes her racial middle location as grayish white. Jasmine states that there is "black and white and there's no gray. And it's funny cause where do I fall? I guess grayish white. Yup, meaning that, I guess I am in the middle, but people, obviously, nobody's ever thought I'm black, ever. I don't think I fall into the series of categories with them either. But I do maintain and just my own culture and keeping up the Puerto Rican culture plus adapting to the American [culture]. So that's why I guess I say I'm grayish white." Jasmine's use of "grayish white" connotes a duller shade of white that best embodies her "white" phenotype and acculturation to American (or white) culture, while remaining firmly grounded in Puerto Rican culture.

The social milieu can also tip the racial middle toward whites. These were youths who grew up in relative isolation from other Latinos (and blacks), in white, middle-class suburban communities. This helps explain why Dario feels that he occupies a racial middle leaning toward white: "I would have to say whites. I guess it's because I have always attended mainly white schools, and most of the friends I have had and still have today are white." For Ignacio, an eighteen-year-old second-generation Mexican who identifies racially as Hispanic, his racial middle tilts toward white because "I hang out more with white people." Not being exposed to blacks led some youths to develop views of a "black lifestyle" based largely on stereotypes. For instance, Heriberto, a twenty-two-year-old second-generation man who identifies racially as Mexican, says he is more distant from "African Americans because some of their lifestyles. I can't see myself living that way." This "lifestyle" included cultural stereotypes that were not based on actual experiences with blacks. Heriberto adds, "My lifestyle and ideas are closest to theirs [whites]." The suburbs insulated these millennials from blacks, resulting in their feelings of distance from blacks and relative closeness to whites.

Rosalinda, a twenty-year-old third-generation Mexican who identifies racially as Hispanic, finds it "really hard" to zero in on her racial position. She states, "I would say that we fall in the middle, but if I had to pick one, I would say white because Mexicans did not deal with nearly as much scrutiny as blacks did. And I guess I lean more toward whites just because I have dated white guys but never black. That's just my personal preference, though. I am not speaking for all Hispanics." Rosalinda recognizes that her individual characteristics, experiences, and preferences move her closer to the white side of the color line, but that does not preclude other Latinos' wavering toward the black side.

Some of those in the racial middle tilting toward white have one white parent. For instance, Sally is a twenty-two-year-old second-generation woman who identifies racially as Mexican and Albanian and who, despite being half white, sees herself as a racial middle who is closer to white. She explains, "Well, I guess it would be the white race 'cause I don't associate anything with the black race. I mean, I've learned about their struggles, but I've never seen it. And I have very few friends [who are black]. Not that I am racist or anything. It just happens that I have very few black friends, and even then, they're not really like black. I don't know if that makes sense. They're more like whitewashed. So I guess I fit in more to the whiter side." Sally feels closer to whites than to blacks mainly because she has "never really been in an environment with them. It's not a choice. It's just the way it happened to be. Like I've never grown up like down the street. My high school wasn't all black. I guess just because I've never really had the opportunity to interact with them as much as anybody else." Sally reasons that her tilting toward white is more a consequence of her lack of interaction with blacks than a result of her half-white parentage.

Social class is another factor that shifts the Latino racial middle toward white. It is not necessarily that these youths see Latinos as a whitening group but that those with middle-class status are often viewed by others as white or as "acting white," even if they themselves do not identify racially as whites. Laura, a twenty-year-old second-generation woman who identifies racially as Mexican, states, "I've been told I act white, but I don't know about Mexicans in general. I guess it would depend on social class." Carlos, a twenty-four-year-old second-generation Mexican Guatemalan who identifies racially as white, offers a more elaborate explanation:

> Oh, I definitely think that there is more of a spectrum, because you know, with Barack Obama, people are saying that he is not black enough or whatever. Or, you know, being a Hispanic in this country, people would tell me "Oh, you are not Hispanic enough, because how come you are talking white?" Because I refuse to use slang, and, some of my friends get mad because I speak proper English, or at least I try to. And so, I would see it more in terms of that spectrum, and for me personally, where I would put myself, because of my family background, and because my parents are educated, and both have high-level degrees, I would be in the middle, or toward the white Latino side of the spectrum.

For Carlos, the designation as white Latino conveys more than color. It reflects his middle-class status, which moves him closer to white privilege than to black marginalization.

Experiences of discrimination also factored into some millennials' claim for a racial middle that tilts toward white. These youths do not identify racially as white but nevertheless locate their racial position as leaning toward white because they do not face the same kind of discrimination as blacks, but neither do they enjoy the privileges of whiteness.

Rick, a twenty-year-old third-generation Mexican who identifies racially as a white Hispanic, says that others see him as white and that he feels closer to both Latinos and whites. He states, "I would say that I, along with those like me, fit within the white dichotomy. We do not face as much discrimination, if any at all, depending on where you grow up. We are just viewed as being more white than black." As Jay, a twenty-eight-year-old third-generation man who identifies racially as Mexican but says people usually think he is Italian, says, "I don't know. If it's black and white, I would say it's gotta be more white than black if you go on stereotypes. Or if not white, then somewhere in the middle. There's no way I could identify with black because I think in terms of, you know, being racist or discriminated against, it's a different world. Black stereotypes do not fit obviously the white stereotypes, and most Mexican people are known as hard workers. Where you have the stereotype of black people being lazy for the most part." Jay, as well as many other Latino millennials, accept stereotypical views of Latinos and blacks that are particularly critical of blacks (see Feagin and Cobas 2014). They also subscribe to the notion of black exceptionalism by viewing blacks as the most disadvantaged group. Blanca, who is a twenty-four-year-old, second-generation Mexican and identifies racially as Hispanic, lays out the dilemma experienced by those who feel they have had it better than blacks but not as good as whites when she says, "I don't feel like I've been discriminated against or anything so . . . I don't know if I would fit in with the white." This feeling that blacks have had it harder while whites have it easier makes it difficult for these Latinos to identify as either blacks or whites.

Identification as a racial middle tilting toward white may also reflect somewhat more access to white privilege relative to blacks. As Carina, a twenty-two-year-old second-generation Mexican who identifies racially as other, expresses in the previous chapter, she has access to some white privilege. She says she falls on the white side of the color line "based on the color of my skin. Based on my education too. Level of education. Just because I see a lot of poorer groups." Carina recognizes that because of their darker skin color, some Latinos do not have access to white privilege, but as a light-skinned Latina, she is privy to some of these advantages. This sentiment echoes Fox and Guglielmo's (2012) argument that positions Latinos as boundary straddlers. In their historical analysis, they found that Latinos have been construed simultaneously as white and nonwhite and that they have had experiences that share commonalities with those of both whites and blacks without being the same as either, thus reflecting a unique process of racialization and racial position as a relevant social category in U.S. society.

Some of these millennials reluctantly acknowledge that they fall closer to the white side of the color line not because of their own identification but because of how the government classifies Latinos as white. Elianna, a twenty-year-old second-generation Mexican who identifies racially as Hispanic and feels most distant from whites, explains, "In terms of the government and their kind of labeling, I would be considered white just because everything that is not black fits into that even though you might be darker. I feel it is very limiting. That dichotomy is not a good representation of race and just people in general. I don't really agree with it, but in forms where the government would place me in other kinds of structures [it] would probably be in the white dichotomy area." While Elianna sees herself as a racial middle who does not fit into either end of the color line, she is aware that "officially" she is pressed into the white side of the color line.

While their attitudes seem to align with the black exceptionalism and the whitening of Latinos, these youths' position as a racial middle tilting toward white has more to do with being able to "pass" as white among strangers, or seeing themselves as disadvantaged in comparison to whites but not as disadvantaged as blacks, or being racialized differently from blacks. Yet these youths feel most distant and alienated from whites, conveying that despite their apparent racial proximity, they are still clearly outside the boundaries of whiteness.

A Racial Middle Tilting toward Black

Defying common assumptions about Latinos' gravitation toward white, almost a quarter of the "racial middle" Latino millennials defined themselves as a racial middle that tilts toward the black side of the color line. Similarly to those whose racial middle tilts toward white, these youths' reasons were partially about their skin color, appearance, or ancestry but mostly about their racialization as minorities, which drew them closer to the black end of the color line. Ana, a twenty-two-year-old second-generation Guatemalan who identifies racially as Latina, states that she would fall "probably in the black. If I got choices, maybe the black. One, I'm a minority, and two, just 'cause I'm darker-skinned, and [three] we don't tend to get the same opportunities as other people." As Frances, a twenty-year-old second-generation Mexican who identifies racially as Latina, states, "Well, I think that there's white, and then our race. I think we fall in with the blacks, or Middle Eastern." This divide between whites and "our race" does not mean they occupy the same racial position; rather, the racial hierarchy is best characterized by a sharper line dividing whites from all other groups.

There are some national origin differences in how these millennials conceptualized Latinos as a racial middle tilting toward black. Most youths who mentioned ancestry, phenotype, or skin color tended to be Puerto Rican or Cuban, while those who focused mainly on shared racial experiences were Mexicans. This is consistent with a previous study in which I found that Puerto Ricans felt closer to blacks because they traced their ancestry partially to Africa or found more cultural commonalities between Puerto Rican and African American cultures, while for Mexicans, the basis of this closeness was their similar experiences of discrimination (Flores-González 1999). For instance, Roberto, a Puerto Rican man who identifies racially as Hispanic, says he falls "in between there. They say we come from black mixed with the Hispanics. I would have to go more toward being black as I'm black skin." Another Puerto Rican, Miguel, aged twenty-six, defines himself racially as Latino but says, "I say more of the black because [of] our ancestry going back has to do more with the Africans. So I say more the black." Still another Puerto Rican, Michael, a twenty-seven-year-old third-generation man who identifies racially as white because he has light skin and defines Latinos as a racial "rainbow," sums all of this up when he says:

We're the rainbow. Specifically, I can say Puerto Ricans but for many Latinos we're the rainbow. I guess my phenotype, what I express on my face is white but my genotype has to be a mixture of everything. My grandmother is black. If we're talking about race as far as black and white, my grandma is black. She is dark as hell. I'm pretty light-skinned, so if you're going to base it just on the way I look, then, yeah, I'm white. But as far as my genotype, as far as what DNA makes me up, I'm different. I'm everything. Every Puerto Rican is too. We're the rainbow. I don't think you can define them as black and white. Whether Puerto Ricans are white, whether Puerto Ricans are black, we're everything.

Being "everything," it is impossible to choose one side of the color line. Besides having a "genotype" that is so mixed that it makes him "everything," Michael understands that his location as a racial middle that leans toward black is based on physical proximity, cultural affinity, and shared racial experiences. He adds:

> I think that they [blacks] have a similar experience to the Puerto Rican experience, and a lot of our art and music is based on, well, you know, a lot of Puerto Rican music comes from Africa, a lot of it is rooted in Africa, like African American music. So I think that I definitely connect a lot with African Americans. Plus growing up I had a lot of black friends. Here in Logan Square, growing up in the eighties and nineties, it was Puerto Ricans and blacks. That's mainly what you had here. And so I thought I connected more with them, based on our experiences growing up, and based on what we've been through. . . . Even though I think that my personal experience here growing up in Chicago is closest to African Americans, more so than Mexican, because of where I grew up, and because of the music that I listened to growing up, and because of the games that I played, I'd still say, yeah, those two groups.

For Michael, his physical proximity, cultural similarities and shared racial experiences as a Latino drive him closer to blacks despite his light skin color.

Some Latino millennials point to the structural dimension of Latino marginality that places them closer to the black experience. Placing herself on the black side of the color line, Elissa, a nineteen-year-old second-generation woman who identifies racially as Mexican, notices the shared disadvantages of Latinos and blacks when saying, "Well, I would say black because we all tend to live in the worst neighborhoods, and we're like segregated basically by our government, and we don't always go to the best schools. We go to the public schools, and we don't always get the best teachers." These youths often lived in the same neighborhoods as blacks and attended school and developed friendships with blacks. The effect of residential and school segregation cannot be overstated here, since which side of the color line these millennials tilted toward had much to do with which group was more proximate physically. Most located themselves toward the bottom of the racial hierarchy because they shared space (in neighborhoods and schools) and experiences of racialization with blacks.

For others, particularly for Mexicans, tilting toward black had mainly to do with a shared minority status. Manuel, a twenty-seven-year-old second-generation Mexican who identifies racially as human and is perceived as Mexican or white, says he is a "middle ground," but he also states that he "would fit in the category of black man." He drives this issue home when he says that the white and black lens diminishes and hides the distinct forms of marginalization of Latinos, Asians, and Native Americans:

Well, in this dichotomy we fall to the wayside, definitely marginalized. I wouldn't want to say more than blacks, but we're marginalized. We're definitely excluded. I mean everything is going to be a black and white issue. It's not a black and white issue. There's Asians and Latinos. There's different ethnicities like Native Americans, and to make it just a black and white issue polarizes it and leaves out this middle ground. Exclusion, I guess . . . when it comes to talking about social issues [it is about] black and white issues. Definitely, I feel that we're not really included. Recently I feel like there's been more because of the immigration issue.

This division of the color line into a white/black binary obscures the fact that nonwhite, nonblack groups also experience exclusion, but in different ways. Latinos share minority status with other nonwhite groups, but each group's experiences are unique and reflective of their particular history of oppression. Growing up in white suburbia, Manuel has many white friends but feels "a little more conscious," especially when he spots a black or "a Mexican kid here in a sea of like white kids. I think I would identify more with the other category, I mean, I don't have any animosity toward whites, unless if it comes off like it is vulgar [and] explicit racism. I try to see it more as a system of social constructs." Recalling a conversation with one of his professors, he concludes that he "would fit into the category of black man. And I think it's because I work with communities of color because I don't hold the traditional

Eurocentric, you know, like ideals, and yeah I would identify more with them [blacks]. I think our people have experienced similar discrimination, the specifics are different but I think general, we're always others. We're always the other category. Excluded, definitely. We don't fit the Eurocentric model."

Arielle, a twenty-one-year-old second-generation woman who identifies racially as Mexican, sums it up when she says that she feels closer to blacks because Latinos and blacks are in the "same boat." Being viewed as "not bad but not good," these youths feel that they do not truly belong among whites. Mary, a nineteen-year-old third-generation woman who identifies racially as Mexican, states, "I think I would be closer to being black than I would to being white because Mexicans are minorities just like blacks. I don't think white people will ever truly accept us either." Also feeling unaccepted, Liz, a twenty-six-year-old second-generation woman who identifies racially as Mexican, explains, "I think society would place me closer to black because of the oppressing natures that the white dichotomy have on the black and Hispanic population. We are seen as outsiders in this country, as someone who does not belong." She is "more comfortable with the black [side of the] dichotomy because they [blacks] deal with a lot of stereotypes and oppressions as well, so I feel that I can relate more to them. . . . I would have to say that the Caucasian ethnicity I feel farther from due to the fact that I think in my lifetime I felt more put down by them on a whole."

While these millennials identify as a racial middle tilting toward black, this identification is not without conflicted feelings that arise as they yearn for privilege. For instance, Yahaira, a twenty-four-year-old second-generation woman who identifies racially as Mexican, locates herself closer to blacks but at the same time tries to put distance between herself and blacks to gain some of the perks she perceives she will get by being closer to whites:

> I would categorize myself more toward the black side of the color line in terms of race. Of course, everyone would like to be more white. They get the advantages in life. But I know that society puts me toward the black side, mainly because of the color of my skin. . . . I feel closer, clearly, to any Hispanic or Latino group. While I'm still a minority, I feel closer to the white side of the spectrum, rather than the black side. Part of this is

how I was brought up, black people are not right. But, it's also how I see it. I do not want to be associated with them in terms of the social and racial aspect, I would rather be associated with the white category. But that does not mean that I am racist toward them. One of my best friends is black. I just have a different idea about where I want to be on the social and political ladder.

Yahaira's narrative conveys these youths' understanding about racial privilege and the disadvantages that identifying as black may pose for them; still, they feel that their racial experiences are closer to those of blacks and thus orient the racial middle toward the black side of the color line.

Rethinking Latinos' Location in the Racial Order

The Latino millennials' narratives presented in this chapter challenge notions about the U.S. racial order as a binary delineated by a sharp color line that places whites in a superior position and blacks in a subordinate position, and assumes that Latinos, based on their racial features, fall on one or the other side. Posing a challenge to this assumption is the fact that only a few of the youths located themselves on the white or black side of the color line and that their narratives are littered with inconsistencies. Simply put, their racial location as white or black does not match their racial identification, nor does it pair with their stated social distance from particular groups. It is therefore faulty to use racial identification as a proxy for racial location. The inconsistency between racial location and racial identification suggests that Latinos' racial location choice is "by default" and is a response to the binary logic that if they do not fall on the black side of the color line, they must fall on the white side and vice versa. That is, they are trying to make sense of a racial rationale that does not reflect their racial reality.

Also trying to make sense of this flawed racial rationale, and posing another critique of it, are the vast majority of youths who identified as a racial middle. At one end are the majority who say that their racial position falls between whites and blacks. These youths pry open this binary by wedging themselves in between and thus turning it from a biracial to a triracial or multiracial order. Next to them are those who seem to conform—although reluctantly and unconvincingly—to the racial binary. These youths say that they do not fall on either side of the color line. At the other end are the youths who refuse to place themselves in the racial order; they see the racial order as flawed but cannot imagine how to reconstitute it to reflect their racial reality.

Although the racial middle is not a new concept, it is largely undertheorized. By digging deeply into the youths' understanding of their racial location, I provide a more intricate conceptualization of the racial middle. First, the youths' narratives contradict notions of the racial middle as a "catchall" category that includes other groups, including Asians—those groups that Bonilla-Silva (2004) calls honorary whites—or as a "transitional stage" on the path to assimilation, such as like Lee and Bean's (2010) social whitening. These youths' responses are in tune with others (e.g., Hitlin, Brown, and Elder 2007; Frank, Akresh, and Lu 2010), who point to Latinos as one of the multiple intermediate categories occupied by Asians, Middle Easterners, and Native Americans. Each of these intermediate categories corresponds to the unique racialization of these nonwhite/nonblack groups. Rather than a one-dimensional hierarchical racial structure, these youths' narratives suggest a hierarchical racial structure wherein group position is based on how each group is racialized along multiple dimensions. Kim's (1999) racial triangulation model serves as a more fitting model for understanding how these Latino millennials think about their racial location. In determining their racial location, these youths invariably made comparisons with other groups. They viewed their racial position as inferior to that of whites, who have access to privilege, and to Asians, who stand out as model minorities. However, they are slightly higher in positioning compared with blacks, with whom they share minority status along the valorization scale. Yet, in the civic ostracism scale, they were lower than any other group (as both white and blacks are indisputable Americans), and although they shared with Asians status as foreigners, it was Latinos who were associated with "illegality."

Second, their narratives show that the Latino racial middle is not a static or uniform intermediate category. While as a group Latinos constitute a racial middle that lies between the white and the black sides of the color line, the location of individuals within the racial middle varies, as some place themselves closer to whites or blacks. This variation depends on individual characteristics—including skin color and social class—as well as their racial experiences. As a result, the racial middle can be divided into three segments: a segment that is located solidly in the middle, one that tilts toward white, and another that tilts toward blacks.

These narratives emphasize the need for the rearticulation of the racial order from one that focuses on a biracial divide based on colorism to one with a multiracial divide based on other variables that affect racialization. In making sense of their racial location, these youths engage in comparisons with other racial groups. Through these comparisons, they come to understand that they are racialized differently from whites and blacks, as well as from other minority groups. Many factors weigh on these comparisons, including skin color and phenotype, cultural and ideological similarities, physical proximity to other groups, social class and access to privilege, and racial experiences. These factors accentuated similarities and differences between the groups, leading them to conceptualize the racial order as nonbinary. Although these factors partly determine Latinos' place in the racial hierarchy, these youths' racial location has much to do with how their Latin American ancestry "others" them as nonwhite and nonblack. Without minimizing the higher frequency and intensity of negative racial experiences of darker-skinned Latinos, it is evident from the narratives of light-skinned Latinos as well as from the narratives of Latinos who have a white parent that they also face frequent and insidious discrimination as they go about their daily lives.

Overall, Latino millennials' narratives point to the inadequacy of the conventional conceptions of the racial order to account for how people actually think of their own and others' racial positions. These conventional ideas are divorced from present-day notions of the racial hierarchy, particularly for Latinos. Being subsumed under ill-fitting categories highlights their racial exclusion from the imagined U.S. society. Claiming a racial middle then reflects their efforts toward racial inclusion.

5

Latinos as "Real" Americans

Latino millennials' narratives convey their reluctance, in many cases, to identify as Americans. This sentiment is expressed by Johnny, a twenty-three-year-old second-generation man who identifies ethnically and racially as Mexican, when he bluntly states, "I don't feel like I am American, I feel like I am Mexican American." Manuel, a twenty-seven-year-old second-generation Mexican, expresses this reluctance by saying, "I'm a citizen. I was born here. So in a strict definition of a citizen, I am a citizen. American? That's up for discussion." Another millennial, Manolo, a twenty-two-year-old second-generation Mexican, sheds light on this reluctance to identify as American when he states, "I don't use 'American' to describe myself because I think others would not. I am a citizen, though. I'm born here in the [United] States. But I think that the word 'American' is not used to describe Mexicans or any other Latinos in this country." Most poignant is the comment made by Diego, a twenty-two-year-old second-generation man who identifies ethnically as Mexican and Latino and racially as Mexican, and struggles to define himself as an American. To him, "American can be anybody. I kind of understand why, the idea behind it, trying to have unity, trying to have everybody be the same or something like that. I say something like that because I'm not even sure what it is, what it's supposed to be. Maybe that's a reflection of how I feel, you know, in this country. I'm not even sure what the hell an American is supposed to be like, you know, and I've been living here twenty-two years, since I was born. So what does that tell you?" Like Diego, these youths denounce the claim to inclusiveness that is central to the American ideal because in practice not everyone is viewed as an American. They hesitate to call themselves Americans because that is neither how others define them nor an identity they can claim without raising eyebrows.

These narratives illustrate what Castles and Davidson (2000) call "citizens who do not belong" and Ngai (2007) labels as "alien citizens" because, despite their political membership—through their birthright citizenship—these youths are not recognized as members of the nation. Their racial and/or ethnic traits—actual or assumed—are the basis for their exclusion. Castles and Davidson argue that when minority groups, such as the youths in this study, are denied cultural membership, this exclusion serves as the basis for their collective—and continuous— identification as ethnics. Their reluctance to identify as Americans or as fully American and their persistence in identifying panethnically can be understood as a reaction to their exclusion from the American imagined community.

At the root of these youths' feeling of marginalization from the nation is the contradiction between the way in which belonging to the American imagined community is defined and the way in which it actually plays out. In principle, "American" signifies cultural membership based on the shared values and ideals that are assumed to characterize American national identity. The rhetoric of civic nationalism or Americanism is embodied in the principles of ethnoculturalism (white, Anglo-Saxon, Protestant heritage), liberalism (the ideal of freedom and opportunity), civic republicanism (the notion of civic responsibility and the common good), and incorporationism (the notion of America as a multiracial/ multicultural nation of immigrants; Schildkraut 2011; Smith 1988). In practice, it is the ideal of ethnoculturalism that bears the most weight and defines who is considered legitimately an American. Theiss-Morse (2009) argues that "who counts" as American continues to go hand in hand with the "true American" prototype, which she describes as white, northern European, and Christian. Borrowing from Benedict Anderson's (2006) notion of the national group as an imagined community, groups that do not fit the "true American" prototype, physically and/or culturally, are not "imagined" as Americans, are easily dismissed as "not quite Americans," and are stripped of the rights, freedom, and equality enjoyed by prototypical Americans (Theiss-Morse 2009; Carbado 2005; Haney Lopez 2006). Those who fail to meet the ethnocultural ideal— physically and/or culturally—are not seen as American regardless of their adherence to American values. Because ideas about both race and culture make up the "ethnocultural" ideal, I favor *ethnoracial ideal* as a more appropriate and true-to-self label. In this chapter, I examine how U.S.-born Latino millennials construct collective notions of national belonging that contest their ethnoracial exclusion and allow them to reimagine themselves as Americans.

Ethnoracial Citizenship

In making sense of the youths' narratives of national belonging and their efforts at rebranding the American identity, two theoretical frameworks are particularly helpful: Rosaldo's (1997) Latino cultural citizenship and Tsuda's (2014) racial citizenship. The Latino cultural citizenship framework poses that in the United States, citizenship and cultural difference are defined as incompatible, and thus it is assumed that one cannot be ethnic and American at the same time or, to put it another way, one cannot be culturally different from the dominant national culture and still be considered an American. Rosaldo (1997) argues that the notion of universal citizenship is predicated on the white male heteronormative subject and the unacknowledged exclusion and marginalization of those who do not conform to—or fit into—this ideal subject. He advances the concept of *cultural citizenship* to account for how marginalized groups develop notions of citizenship that subvert this dominant ideology. Rosaldo and Flores (1997, 57) define cultural citizenship as "the right to be different (in terms of race, ethnicity, or native language) with respect to the norms of the dominant national community, without compromising one's right to belong, in the sense of participating in the nation-state's democratic process."

Studies using Rosaldo's cultural citizenship framework show that through the use of counterideologies, Latinos seek to disrupt the dominant narratives and expand the notion of citizenship by asserting their right to belong to the nation despite these cultural differences (Benmayor 2002; Flores 2003; Rosaldo and Flores 1997; Silvestrini 1997). Cultural citizenship then provides Latinos with a means to claim, legitimize, and assert their Americanness, while at the same time redefining and transforming what it means to be an American. Cultural citizenship also allows Latinos to construct what Benmayor (2002) calls an *integrated subjectivity* that bridges their multiple worlds by incorporating their cultural ideology and practices in their claims for rights and belonging. That is, Latinos take those very cultural logics and practices that marginalize them and turn them into tools for claiming, affirming, and transforming what it means to be American in a way that incorporates their national and their ethnic identities (Benmayor 2002). Latinos, then, question their exclusion by offering an alternative vision of belonging based on American ideals and values: one in which they can have both a strong ethnic identification and a strong attachment to the nation (Silvestrini 1997). In doing so, Latinos claim cultural citizenship as they seek to move from the fringes to inside the boundaries of the imagined American community, as they ultimately claim a place at the table as equals (Benmayor 2002).

Although most of the work on Latino cultural citizenship focuses on immigrants who have obvious cultural differences, I found that among the U.S.-born youths in this study, cultural differences were not always palpable as much as they were assumed. For many, it is their "race" or physical attributes that deem them not American, even in the absence of cultural traits. Tsuda (2014) poses that third- and subsequent-generation ethnic minorities who are not "ethnic" but rather culturally assimilated to American culture—such as the Japanese Americans he studied—are more likely to engage in what he calls *racial citizenship* rather than in cultural citizenship, as their exclusion is based on racial difference. While Tsuda acknowledges that Rosaldo's initial conceptualization of cultural citizenship accounted for racial differences, he argues that its operationalization has focused solely on cultural difference. While I share Tsuda's concern, I find that his focus on racial difference fails to capture the symbiotic nature of race and ethnicity that is implied—although not applied—in Rosaldo's framework. I pose that racial difference often triggers the assumption of cultural difference, and that ethnic markers such as surnames can also trigger assumptions of cultural difference even in the absence of actual physical or cultural difference. Given this race-ethnicity symbiosis, I merge the cultural and racial citizenship frameworks and relabel it *ethnoracial citizenship* as racial traits and cultural traits both signal non-Americanness.

Using an ethnoracial citizenship framework, this chapter shows how these youths do not passively accept their exclusion. On the contrary, they actively contest the limiting definitions set forth by the dominance of an ethnoracial ideal that rule them out as members of the polity based on their race and/or cultural traits. Four patterns emerged from the data. First, these youths denounce the ethnoracial criteria attached to the notion of being an American. Second, their contestation employs familiar tropes aligned with the ideals of American civic nationalism and emphasize their commonality with fellow Americans. These tropes include citizenship, freedom, opportunity, and patriotism. Third, their contestation also employs counternarratives that emphasize the ethnoracial makeup that distinguishes them—but at the same time makes them more American. These counternarratives include multiculturalism and intercontinentalism. Fourth, they develop an integrated subjectivity that offers a new vision of what it is to be an American that does not require shedding their ethnic heritage. Through their narratives, these youths redefine, assert, and ultimately seek to transform what it means to be an American.

Contesting the American Ethnoracial Ideal

At the heart of the Latino millennials' refusal to identify as American is the ethnoracial definition of "American" as white Anglo-Saxon Protestant. Martha, a twenty-seven-year-old second-generation Mexican, stated in no uncertain terms that American "is a label that was created to categorize people who follow certain traditions in the United States, mainly Anglo-Saxon, Protestant, and male. I really don't think that that term ['American'] means much to me. I mean I normally would not say that I am American." The conflation of "American" with this ethnoracial ideal is illustrated by Raúl, a twenty-one-year-old second-generation Mexican who identifies racially as indigenous:

> Many people associate American as somebody who is born within this country of immigrants, but American is just an ideology. And there's many types of, levels of, what is American. There's an ideal, I guess. Based on when this country was illegally founded by Caucasian culture and people. So that would be the ideal people who would fit that description. And so anybody else who's different, with different race or culture, and who does not fit the description, or doesn't descend from a British, or European culture, I guess it would take down their qualifications for being American, like true Americans. This society has mainly been constructed and authored by European culture. I guess American, ideally, would be anybody who is British or European, and comes to settle in what they call the new world. To come and occupy, and benefit from the land here. So

> I think that, ideally, American is somebody who is accepted by society, and for their culture and identity, and beliefs—which is often you have to be white or prescribe to white culture in order to be accepted in society.

Like Diego in his narrative presented earlier, Raúl addresses the contradiction between the ideal of inclusiveness that "American" represents and its actual exclusiveness. Raúl explains that the term "American" applies fully to people of European ancestry—or whites—who fit the American prototype. Those who are not descendants of Europeans—like himself—do not meet the racial and cultural "qualifications for being American, like true Americans," and fall on the lower rungs of the "many types of, levels of, what is American." Raúl traces this definition of American to the occupation, settlement, and domination by whites that led to the normalization of American as white such that "you have to be white or prescribe to white culture in order to be accepted." More to the point, Danny, a twenty-one-year-old second-generation man who identifies racially as Latino and Mexican, says that even those Latinos who want to call themselves white "will always be seen as Mexican. . . . Because of the color of their skin. . . . Well, they are not Caucasian. They don't look it, talk it, so they wouldn't be seen as fully white. They'll always be a 'wannabe white' Mexican or Puerto Rican." For Danny, a Latino can only be a "wannabe white" because Latinos "will always be seen as Mexican." As these youths suggests, Latinos are a different—and presumably lesser and nonwhite—type of American.

In addition to race (white), ancestry (European), and culture (Anglo-Saxon), these youths also point to class privilege as another component of the American ethnoracial ideal. Daniel, a twenty-two-year-old second-generation Costa Rican who identifies racially as American, says, "If you were to base it purely on color, American is a white person. You know, it's very much the truth, and if you were to drive around the outskirts of Illinois, even, that's all who you'd run into—suburban white people." Implied in Daniel's reference to "suburban white people" is the racial (white) and middle-class (suburban) notion tied to the ethnoracial ideal of American. Coupling American with whiteness brings up white racial and middle-class statuses inherent in the American ideal. Ricky, a seventeen-year-old second-generation Mexican, explains why he does not feel "like an American":

I guess I think an American is white, though, like I don't think I really feel like an American. I feel like a Mexican. I know I live in America and I know I was born here, but I feel separate from Americans, I guess. . . . I don't know, it's just like Mexicans are different than all of the people I think are Americans, or say they are Americans. Americans, I don't know, they're like the managers and like the waiters at restaurants. Mexicans are somewhere in the back all the time. I don't think Mexicans are really Americans. I don't really feel like an American.

Coming from working-class families, and not fitting the ethnoracial ideal either racially or culturally, very few of the Latino millennials can then measure up to the white, Anglo-Saxon middle-class standard of American, conveyed in the image of the white family in a suburban house with a white picket fence.

To top it off, Americans are also defined as nonimmigrants. That is, Americans are imagined not only as people of European descent, white, and middle class but also as nonimmigrants whose families date back several generations in the United States. Mariann, a twenty-five-year-old second-generation Puerto Rican, states that "the term [American] means white European that have a couple generations here. . . . People that have a house or some form of value. . . . White people." Implied by a "couple of generations here" is the lack of recent immigrant background coupled with "white European" and "people that have a house," all of which denote the merging of race, ancestry, culture, and middle-class status as a proxy for American. These youths' narratives line up with those given by Bloemraad's (2013) respondents, who also equated American with racial majority status, affluence, and privilege—dimensions that excluded them from claiming Americanness.

Accustomed to not being seen as Americans because they do not fit the ethnoracial ideal, these youths experience a shock when they are identified as Americans outside of the United States. Nikki, a twenty-two-year-old second-generation woman who identifies ethnically and racially as Mexican, explains this paradox when saying, "I feel that I am more Mexican than American. Being here in the U.S. you're automatically Mexican. If I was to go to Mexico, I'm not Mexican. I am American. Being here I feel like it's not really . . . you're not titled as you're American. Maybe with the government I guess you would be American because you were born here, but that is as far as it goes." For Nikki, calling herself American in the United States is absurd because legally she may be an American, but "you're automatically [seen as] Mexican," but outside of the United States, she is blatantly American. Mike, a twenty-eight-year-old second-generation Colombian who identifies racially as Hispanic, expresses a similar feeling:

> In this country I think you are from somewhere else and you are together with everyone else that is around you. But, I am Colombian here, but when I go to Colombia, I am American. So no one is really American here unless they leave the country. . . . Citizens, I don't think anyone is an American because everyone came from somewhere else. You are not American even if you were born here, your family is still from somewhere else unless you are Native American. . . . I am Colombian because that is where my parents are from, but I am also American because I was born here. But, I am a Colombian by nature, and when I leave the country, I will be American.

Mike and Nikki are just two of the many Latino millennials who spoke of their experience as Americans when abroad.

Yet, more shockingly, when these youths are abroad, they often discover just how American they actually are. Manuel, who in the opening paragraph of this chapter expressed his reluctance to identify as American, is among those who was surprised to find that although in the United States these youths' Americanness is often doubted, outside of the United States, they are glaringly so. Manuel says, "I don't fit the idea [of American] because the idea is a very Eurocentric idea. But, I mean, if we broaden it and try not to be so specific, like you know when I travel, when I leave the country, when I went to Mexico it's like people knew I was American. You know, my tattoos are American, my shoes are American, my clothes are American, my accent in Spanish is American. And my English, you know, I speak mostly without an accent so they hear me speak and they see me, they're like 'Americano,' you know, American." While abroad, Manuel stands out as unmistakably American, with his visible tattoos, clothing styles, and "American" accent when speaking Spanish as telltale signs. Yet, in the United States, he is not unmistakably American.

Whatever hope these Latino millennials had of fitting into the parental homeland quickly vanishes upon visiting. They realize that they are not as ethnically authentic as they had thought, and it dawns on them just how American they really are. For Sofia, going to Mexico "just makes me feel really American." In telling about his experiences in Mexico, Manuel states that "it was definitely a connection, an experience, and it definitely made me realize how Mexican I really am not. You know because people here will be like 'You're Mexican' or 'This is Mexican.' The Mexicans here, not only the Americans, the Euro-Americans but the Mexican Americans will be like 'This is what a Mexican is.' And then you go there and you're like 'No, you got it all wrong. You think that's Mexican.' But people down there [don't consider it Mexican]." For Manuel, as for many of the youths, travel to the parental homeland brings the realization that they've "got it all wrong"—that is, that what they had assumed to be Mexican is not really Mexican. Living in the United States, these youths held essentialist and often static notions of cultural authenticity that do not conform to cultural norms, to cultural change, or to cultural diversity in the parental homeland. These youths experience what others refer to as "ni de aquí, ni de allá," or a feeling that they do not belong fully in either place.

American Tropes and National Identity

Because they do not fit the ethnoracial criteria attached to notions of the American subject, these youths engage in the contestation of their exclusion. Demonstrating their understanding of American national ideology, they deploy familiar American tropes to assert themselves as members of the nation. Like Bloemraad's (2013) respondents, these youths form notions of belonging that emphasize their U.S. citizenship and their subscription to perceived American civic ideals. Latino millennials in my study employed the tropes of citizenship, freedom, opportunity, and patriotism. In the following pages, I discuss how, through the use of these tropes, Latino millennials emphasize their similarities, as well as the differences that make them particularly American, or at least a type of American. I also pay attention to intervening factors—such as gender, educational level, and racial identification—that may skew individuals to deploy particular tropes.

Not fitting the American ethnocultural ideal (white, middle-class, and suburban), these youths seek to redefine Americanness by equating it to citizenship. The use of citizenship as proof of Americanness is widespread, as there were no discernible gender, educational, or racial identification differences among the youths engaged in this form of contestation. These youths take on a more pragmatic stance that emphasizes birthright citizenship as the primary prerequisite for being American, and point to their birthright citizenship as incontrovertible proof of their Americanness. Alluding to his earlier comment that tied American to whiteness and middle-class status, Daniel adds:

> For me it's the people who were born on American soil. But I know that when most people think about that term, they picture a stereotypical white person, you know, fair and middle-class and suburban. . . . But I think that people who contribute to this country and who seek to improve themselves when it comes to their education and career should be allowed to become American citizens. But truly, for me, you are most American if you're born on the American soil. [And] based on what the law says, because I was born in the United States of America, I am an American. I mean, I can still run for the presidency. Just based on that concept, that rule, I am an American.

As Daniel points out, American is imagined as "the stereotypical white person" who is "fair[-skinned] and middle-class and suburban." And while he calls on the American values of liberalism ("seek to improve themselves") and civic republicanism ("contribute to this country"), ultimately, for him, it is birthright citizenship ("born on American soil") that proves that "you are most American." Likewise, Adamaris, a twenty-one-year-old second-generation Guatemalan who identifies racially as Latina, emphasizes this legal angle when stating that American means "that you were born in this country. . . . I was born here and I'm a U.S. citizen so . . . by law I'm an American." Other youths also identify themselves as Americans because of their U.S. birth. Justin, a twenty-three-year-old second-generation Mexican who identifies racially as Latino, states that an American is "anybody who was born in this country within the borders of the United States of America." Also stressing U.S. birth, Samantha, a twenty-two-year-old third-generation Mexican

Puerto Rican who identifies as white, says that Americans are "people who are citizens here. You know, that is what America means to me. If you're from this country, you're an American." Youths like Adamaris, Justin, and Samantha link American to birthright citizenship. This pragmatic—and legal—approach to Americanness was also observed by Bloemraad (2013), particularly among U.S.-born participants who, despite invoking other American ideals, ultimately relied on citizenship to prove their Americanness.

Many youths extend this legal definition of American to include naturalized citizens. Araceli, a twenty-seven-year-old second-generation Mexican who identifies racially as Mexican, states that "an American is a person who was born in the U.S. or has resided here for many years and has become a citizen." Yet, Americanness is not limited to citizens, as some youths extend it also to noncitizens. Martha expands on her previous ethnocultural definition of American to include legal permanent residents as American when she states, "It can be anyone that's living in the United States that can identify as American. But then again, it's also takes into consideration someone's legality in the United States. So, whether you are a U.S. citizen, or you're legally here as a resident. . . . If I were to place myself within that definition, I am an American because I am a U.S.-born citizen." Although Americanness seems to imply legality, some push the limits of this equation by also including noncitizens— and presumably undocumented immigrants. For instance, Marina, a twenty-three-year-old second-generation Mexican who identifies racially as Hispanic, adds that an American is "anyone born or raised here, anyone living here."

Despite claiming Americanness through their citizenship, these youths know that they are not considered Americans—especially by whites. Rosario, a twenty-four-year-old second-generation woman who identifies racially as Mexican, says, "To me, the term 'American' means white man. . . . Well Americans are supposed to be everyone living in America, or have citizenship, but everyone doesn't get treated like an American. . . . I fit in this definition because I have citizenship, but lots of time when the issue of immigration comes up and I'm around my white friends, they sometimes joke about me being an immigrant or not really American." Here, Rosario starts by connecting American to the ethnoracial ideal and to legality. The predominance of the ethnoracial ideal comes through when she implies that citizenship does not guarantee that she will be seen and treated as an American, even by those who know she is U.S.-born. Although Rosario dismisses her white friends' comments as jokes, they are intended to remind her of her exclusion as a national subject.

Instances of white supremacy are not missed on Javier, a twenty-four-year-old second-generation Mexican who identifies as Latino, when he exclaims, "I mean, in an ideal world, I would tell you that all that live here are Americans. I would say that America is the melting pot and that we all are part of it. But that is not true. Americans are the elite of the race, and they dictate who is American and who is not." Similar portrayals of whites as the "elite of the race" and as those who determine "who counts" were expressed by other Latino millennials, as well as their sense that birthright citizenship is not a proxy for American. As a result, many stress their engagement with the American ideals of liberalism and civic republicanism to assert their Americanness.

Latino millennials also play up their Americanness by emphasizing their adoption of the liberal ideals of freedom and opportunity. Similarly to those who emphasized their citizenship to stake a claim as members of the nation, there were no significant gender, educational, or racial identification differences among those deploying the American liberal trope of freedom in order to prove their Americanness. For these youths, the trope of freedom is an essential component of Americanness. As Kate, a twenty-three-year-old second-generation Mexican who identifies racially as human and Hispanic, exclaims, "Freedom! Freedom is a big issue for Americans. Everything is about being free. There is all the talk about the war and all the different sides about it, and I think it's, just, Americans are obsessed with freedom." Defining freedom as a "big issue" and an obsession, Kate casts it as a fundamental precept of American national identity. Blanca, a twenty-four-year-old second-generation Mexican who identifies racially as Hispanic, also thinks that being American is "just having that freedom that other people don't have. It's very important. I think that's the most important American thing—freedom." To these youths, freedom is an essential value that characterizes American national identity, and it is a value that they share.

When speaking about freedom, these youths zero in on freedom of speech without fear of retaliation, which they say distinguishes the United States from other countries. José, a twenty-eight-year-old second-generation Mexican Cuban who identifies racially as Latino, states, "What makes someone an American would mostly be the idea of the freedom that you have." He goes on to explain that in "other countries you can't really speak your voice. If you wrote something in an article, about a political figure . . . they would hunt you down. Punish you. Punish your family. Here, you can speak about anybody." José is not alone, as others shared this notion of freedom as part of American exceptionalism. Brian, a twenty-two-year-old second-generation Mexican Irish man who identifies racially as American, also sees freedom as a particular American characteristic that is not found everywhere. To him, "What it means to be American comes back to the whole freedom of choice thing that separates us from every other country. We have choices no one else does. We can say our President sucks, and no one else can. So, we have choice and we have freedom of opinion. . . . [Americans] accept someone disagreeing with [them] and honoring their position whether they are racists or not . . . rather than killing them over it like in other countries—like in Afghanistan." Brian buys into the trope of American exceptionalism by believing that Americans have freedom of speech and can state their opinion without fear for their lives, even if their comments are critical of the government or offensive to others, unlike the censure that he believes exists in other countries.

Latino millennials also pair Americanness with the liberal trope of opportunity. Youths who engaged with the trope of opportunity tended to identify racially by ethnic origin and/or panethnically, and while all viewed the United States as a land of opportunity, there was a slight difference in how young men and women measured success. Expressions of "America as the land of opportunity" and the "American dream" are common in these youths' narratives, particularly in reference to their families' immigration stories. Laura, a twenty-year-old second-generation Mexican who identifies her race as Mexican, links her parents' motivation to migrate to the opportunities available for their children in the United States. For Laura, "America is just like an opportunity for us, and I don't know if it's because my parents that's how they spoke of it as 'America is your opportunity to succeed in life the way we didn't.' So my parents didn't have the opportunity, so they gave us the opportunity." Laura, like many millennials, is aware of her parents' struggles and lack of opportunity in Mexico. Taking their parents' country of origin as their point of reference, these youths view the United States as the land of opportunity. Similarly, Manolo, who at the beginning of this chapter expressed his reluctance to call himself American, explains the promise of opportunity through his family's immigrant story when he says, "Being American means that you have the right to get whatever you work hard for. That is why my parents came to the States, for my family to be able have more in life. In Mexico, there are no jobs like here, no chance because of our government. We were not able to get anything that would allow us to get ahead. By coming to America and becoming American, my parents thought we could have all this and more by going to school here, learning the language, getting smart and helping them when we get good jobs." For Manolo's family, the United States represents social mobility for those willing to work hard, opportunities that simply did not exist in Mexico. Sharing the ethic of hard work, his family fits the American trope of pulling oneself up by one's bootstraps.

Many Latino millennials shared the belief in the American promise of social mobility for those who work hard. Gonzalo, a twenty-two-year-old second-generation man who identifies racially as Mexican, makes explicit reference to the American dream and to his will and drive to succeed as proof of his Americanness:

> [American is] someone who does what they can in order to achieve whatever goal. It doesn't matter what the color of their skin is. It's the goal that they seek out and hope to obtain it. Like, they'll do whatever it is in order to achieve the American dream. Anyone that can achieve the American dream is considered an American in my eyes. . . . I try to make a better future for myself. I try to set down some goals. I am a person that lives in this country. I do want to be successful in life and have all the good things. And I guess that's what makes me American.

In his narrative, Gonzalo downplays the significance of race as a defining American trait by stressing that "it doesn't matter what the color of their skin is," insisting that "what makes me American" is his pursuit of opportunities. Similarly, Diana, a nineteen-year-old third-generation Mexican who identifies as Hispanic, believes that what characterizes

Americans is taking "advantage of the opportunities that are available" and wanting to "achieve more than they're handed." The belief that anything is possible if one works hard resonates with Katerina, a nineteen-year-old second-generation Ecuadorian who identifies racially as Hispanic, as she adds that "the term American means being able to have the privilege to accomplish anything you want in life" and, more concretely, "being able to attend school, given freedom of speech, and to vote." For these youths, their Americanness is asserted by their pursuit of these opportunities and their promise of social mobility.

Some youths went beyond the pursuit of opportunities by accentuating their Americanness through their accomplishments. Gender interacted with how youths viewed success, with young women pointing to their educational achievement as proof of their Americanness while young men were less enthusiastic. Similar to Nancy López (2002), I found that young women viewed education as an avenue for social mobility and as a means for economic independence and self-sufficiency. Lisa, a twenty-five-year-old second-generation Colombian who identifies her race as "none-Hispanic," is proud of putting herself through college. She says, "To me [American] means being independent and helping your community just like being independent and successful bringing yourself up and having that opportunity." Likewise, Sarah, a twenty-one-year-old second-generation woman who identifies racially as Mexican, sees herself reflected in the American dream. To her, an American is "anyone who has lived here and has taken on the way of American life, but others believe its people who are citizens and have the right to vote. . . . I'd say I'm American. I was born here. I'm almost done with college. I want a good-paying job with benefits." Like Lisa, Sarah and the other young women in my study do not hold on to the American dream naively. Their experiences at school and at work remind them that as Latinas, they are subject to discrimination. Yet their gender shelters them from the more frequent and intense racial experiences of surveillance and overt discrimination that are typical among young men and that contribute to their bleaker outlooks on the promise of opportunity (see chapter 2).

While buying into the tropes of opportunity, young men were particularly critical of the limits of these ideals in practice. They know that some people are more equal than others, and that Latinos often hold the short end of the stick. These youths—and particularly young men—insert race into an equation that results in greater disadvantage for Latinos. Pablo, a sixteen-year-old second-generation student who identifies racially as Mexican American, cautions that the idea that "you are treated equally and also like you have opportunities" is inconsistent because these opportunities are "usually just [for] white people. African Americans too. . . . Probably us too, but not as much." Pablo sees a hierarchy of opportunity, with whites reaping the perks, African Americans enjoying some benefits, and Latinos getting the crumbs. More poignant is the view espoused by Jesús, a twenty-one-year-old second-generation Mexican who identifies racially as Latino. He sees "empty promises . . . because you're led to believe that if you work hard that you can become anything you want. It's a lie. You can work as hard as you want here, get treated unfairly, and never be able to get the things you want because of the racist system here." Jesús's scathing critique of the broken and unfulfilled promise of the American dream is also raised by Javier, who earlier denounced the notion of the American melting pot as a fallacy. Javier explains that "American to me means opportunities at your own risk. . . . Well, I think a lot of people, including myself and my family, thought of America as the land of the free, but we soon found out that there is a lot of discrimination that comes with it. There are really hard times here. I guess in the grand scheme of things, we are better off here, but let me tell you, it wasn't easy." These young men's narratives—including Javier's—do not deny that there are more opportunities in the United States, but they point to what they see as a rigged system that favors particular racial groups. As Javier's account shows, discrimination makes the American dream harder to pursue and impossible to achieve. While these young men praise the ideals of opportunity, they know that in practice these are not distributed equally, and that whites receive a disproportionate share of opportunities. For them, being less than equal within the racial order contributes to their feelings of being less American.

Many Latino millennials also subscribe to American ideals of civic republicanism by emphasizing the tropes of social responsibility and the common good—and in particular their patriotism. Although there were no discernible gender or educational differences, most youths who deployed the patriotic trope identify racially as Latinos or Hispanics. These youths believe that the qualifying characteristic of American is the willingness to contribute to society. This point was stressed by Elianna, a twenty-year-old second-generation Mexican who identifies racially as Hispanic, who thinks that an American is "someone who provides for this country. That gives the country revenue. That helps the country continue because that's kind of what all Americans do. They pay taxes. They're contributing to society and to the growth of our nation, and I feel like someone who does that is in my opinion considered American because they're doing all that they can for this country, and no matter whether they agree with their morals or whatever it is, they essentially are giving something to this country, and that's what's important." Notice that Elianna uses action verbs such as "provides," "gives," "helps," "contributing," and "doing" to emphasize a generalized sense—and active fulfillment—of duties and responsibilities that she believes are the trademarks of Americanness.

Among these duties, these youths include knowing about American culture and history. For Juan, a twenty-three-year-old second-generation Cuban who identifies as Latino, "it's about being raised here and knowing the American culture." The importance of understanding what American stands for was shared by Amanda, a twenty-two-year-old second-generation Mexican Polish who identifies as Hispanic, who states, "I honestly think that being American means not only being a citizen but actually understanding where America came from and what it stands for today. . . . I love the fact that I am an American. The diversity and freedom of our nation brings people together, and I love being a part of it." Nick, a nineteen-year-old third-generation Cuban who identifies as Hispanic, sums up this feeling when he says that American is "someone who devotes their life and everything they do to this country, not just the fact that they were born here. . . . I feel I'm an American. I pay my taxes just like everyone else in this country, so I should deserve all the same rights and privileges that everyone deserves." In saying that he "should deserve all the same rights and privileges," Nick is implying that despite contributing to society, he does not get his fair share.

Another way in which concern with the common good is manifested is in having pride in and love for the country. As David, a twenty-four-year-old second-generation man who identifies racially as Mexican, sums up, an American is "someone who is a U.S. citizen and loves the

U.S.A." Likewise, Sally, a twenty-two-year-old second-generation Mexican Albanian who identifies as Latina, said that being American "just means having pride for the country you live in. You know even if you come from somewhere else, as long as you're here, you know you have pride for being an American." More poignant is a comment by Rick, a twenty-year-old third-generation Mexican who identifies racially as white Hispanic and believes that being an American is about loving and defending the country. Rick believes that "American means someone that is proud to be from the U.S. and shows this pride when necessary. They do what they are supposed to in terms of being American. . . . All those that are proud of the U.S. and are from the U.S. I think that anybody can be an American if they believe they are and if they have their citizenship, and perform their duties to our country. . . . I fit in because I am proud. I am American. I am not scared to show my pride, even when many others have things against America." For Rick, standing by your country "even when many others have things against America" proves that you are American. These youths contrast their love for the country by pointing to others' hollow patriotism. Jasmine, a twenty-three-year-old third-generation Puerto Rican who identifies as human, says, "When I think of American, I think of those who are straight up like riding down the street with their American flags and have no idea what it is. They don't care. They have so much pride in it." As Jasmine cautions, patriotism is not about flying the flag and cannot exist without having a full understanding of its meaning.

These narratives show that Latino millennials often imagine themselves as being more American than those who fit the American ethnoracial ideal. These youths recognize that they may not fit the ethnoracial profile, but their values and actions align with other American ideals. Saúl, a twenty-five-year-old second-generation Mexican who identifies as Hispanic, brings together the tropes of patriotism, freedom, opportunity, and social responsibility that Latinos called on when asserting their Americanness:

American means a few things. American is a term that can be used for someone that is born here. American is when you are proud to call the United States your home. American is the belief in the many great people of all types of races, color, gender, and beliefs that make this country not perfect but great. American is a sense of pride and even though we may not like what our leaders chose for us, we, the people who make this country, do have a good heart. American is believing in the people and the American dream and doing your part to make your dream a reality. People who want to help this country prosper by doing good. . . . I am American because I love what we are supposed to stand for. I was born here. I know there is a lot of good in this country, unfortunately, a few ignorant and powerful people give us a bad name and they make us look bad. I believe in the American dream because I am still attending school and will God willing achieve my goal soon.

Like Saúl, Dave, a twenty-two-year-old third-generation Puerto Rican who was the only participant to identify ethnically and racially as American, brings together the tropes of freedom, patriotism, opportunity, and responsibilities when he says, "I think [American] means that you have freedom, patriotism, things of that nature. . . . I think anyone who has lived here for a long time should be considered an American. Someone who contributes to society in some way. Whether it is helping someone out, or just doing their job in the world. You work hard. If you were here for most of your life, I would say that you're an American." Despite deploying these tropes, for these youths, it is the mere fact of living in the United States that should make one American. Using these tropes, Latino millennials then seek to insert themselves into the national group. Although some dabble with a critique of a rigged system that favors whites while still asserting their belonging, others offer a more critical reading on what it means to be an American by offering counternarratives on belonging.

Counternarratives on Belonging

In addition to engaging in narratives that reassert their Americanness through their birthright citizenship and their shared American ideals of liberalism and civic republicanism, Latino millennials deploy counternarratives using the incorporationism trope of multiculturalism and the trope of intercontinentalism to contest the limited meaning of Americanness. Most of the youths who engaged with the trope of multiculturalism identified racially as Latino or Hispanic, and there were no noticeable gender or educational differences. Just as some of the youths quoted in the previous section saw themselves as more worthy and deserving than those who take their Americanness for granted, these youths think that they embody Americanness more than white Americans *because* they are both American and Latino.

Deploying the multiculturalism trope, these millennials turn the ethnoracial ideal of the white Anglo-Saxon Protestant American on its head. Santos, a seventeen-year-old second-generation Mexican who identifies racially as Latino, points to the multicultural nature of the nation when he says that "the United States of America to me means like the whole world because it's like all kinds of races [that] live in America." Although Laura stated earlier that "America is your opportunity," she also speaks to the contradiction of a multicultural nation where the national subject continues to be imagined as white. She says, "An American is like anyone who lives here basically, but most importantly it's like multicultural because like sometimes people think American is like white, you know, 'those [whites] are Americans.' But in reality it's like anyone who lives here and has the opportunity to live like we do is American." Sally previously defined American as having "pride for the country," but she also recognizes the inconsistency between the American trope of multiculturalism and the persistent ethnoracial ideal that narrows the definition of American:

> I speak English, I eat burgers, I eat fries. I celebrate Independence Day. I see, like, summer, some guy on a beach, cooking with a little grill you know. Shorts and sandals, blasting some oldies station or something. I mean, I guess you know someone who has been surrounded by the culture so much that they don't even know anything other than that. Like they don't associate anything with Latin culture or black culture and [they are] kind of just stuck in their ways. . . . I mean, I don't, I dunno. I feel like I'm an American 'cause I was born here and I celebrate the holidays, but I have a more diverse understanding of other cultures.

Sally is aware that the prevalent image of the American (a white middle-aged male) looks nothing like her, yet unlike this image, she embodies multiculturalism: her Americanization is implied by cultural markers (English, burgers and fries, and Independence day), while her multiculturalism comes through in her "more diverse understanding of other cultures."

Like Sally, given their multicultural background, these youths feel that they—more than the prototypical American—embody Americanness. Christine, an eighteen-year-old second-generation Mexican who identifies racially as Hispanic, exclaims, "America is made up of so many different cultures, it's kind of like everyone. Anyone can be an American.... There's different languages, even though it's not accepted. [It is] just generally multicultural . . . because everybody is mixed. Everyone is different. There's not one [single type of] American. I'm multicultural. I grew up here in Chicago, and I know Chinese, Korean, Japanese, Italian, black people. I know people of different races and interact with them. We're all multicultural. I'm multicultural." Christine feels that she embodies Americanness not only because she is both Mexican and American but also because she interacts with and understands people from different ethnic and racial backgrounds. Similarly, Bibiana, a twenty-year-old second-generation Mexican who identifies racially as Hispanic, says, "I think being American is just that you can assimilate into your society and reach out to people of all cultures, not just your own."

Here, embodying Americanness is about these millennials' understanding of other cultures. Octavio, a twenty-year-old second-generation Mexican who identifies racially as Hispanic, states, "For me, being a true American is accepting other cultures. Because that's what America is when you think about it. It's a big melting pot. And we are all the same, trying to achieve the same dream." This sentiment was also expressed by Eric, a twenty-one-year-old third-generation Brazilian Puerto Rican who identifies racially as Puerto Rican and who says that American "means to have citizenship in the U.S. and to be able to understand mainstream American culture or any other aspect of American culture because America has many different cultures of its own within its society. I feel an American is anyone who feels that America is their home regardless of any other such factors. I am an American, and my girlfriend is an American, but we both follow extremely different cultures in American culture alone. But I feel she is my equal, and we are both equally American. There is nothing wrong with this." While, as a Latino, Eric does not fit the ethnoracial ideal, his embodiment of multiculturalism is what makes him "equally American" and on a par with his white—and legitimately American—girlfriend.

Aside from using the term "multiculturalism," I found that a surprisingly large number of Latino millennials engaged in a counternarrative that denounces the appropriation of the term "American" by emphasizing its broader intercontinental meaning. My analysis shows that the youths who use this counternarrative tend to be college students or college graduates, but most notably, these are the youths who identified racially as human. Although initially I dismissed the "human" answer to the race question as frivolous, it took on a significant meaning when paired with these millennials' critique of the term "American." In their refusal to choose a race—or at least their reluctance to engage with racial or ethnic terminology—they voice a more profound critique of exclusion and marginality.

To these youths, the term "American" does not apply solely to people from the United States. They argue that "American" refers to anyone who lives in the Americas—North, Central, or South. Jacques, a twenty-nine-year-old second-generation man who identifies ethnically and racially as Mexican French biracial, states, "To me American is anyone born within either the North or South American continents. I do not consider U.S. citizens to be the only Americans in existence. There is North America and South America, and all those who reside in its countries in my opinion are considered to be Americans. . . . I am American, I was born, raised, and live in the North American continent." For Jacques, American refers to people from North and South America.

In addition to applying the term "American" to all people in the American continents, these youths also denounced what they view as the appropriation of this term by the United States. Teresa, a twenty-one-year-old second-generation Mexican Argentinian who identifies racially as human, plays out this counternarrative when she states that "'American' is just a term that white people made up to define who they are by where they live. . . . [But American is really] anyone that lives in the Americas. . . . I am an American because I live in this continent." Once again, Manuel explains his reluctance to identify as American when he provides what he believes is the more accurate definition of American (someone from the Americas), with the popular definition as someone from the United States. To Manuel, American means the following:

Born in the Americas. Yeah, that's how it should be defined, but I guess how it is defined is someone born in the United States. But American, Bolivians are Americans, and Central Americans and Canadians are Americans. If you want to get specific, I guess we're talking people from the United States. Do you want me to define it culturally? It's like European, you know. It's all-encompassing, but here we've made it specific. I guess someone from the United States with that definition that we use, this continent and this country, then an American would be someone from the United States.

Manuel denounces the territorial and cultural definition that limits American to the United States, while espousing American as an intercontinental identity that includes the inhabitants of North, Central, and South America.

These youths also trace the appropriation of the term "American" and its adoption as a national identity by the United States. Michael, a twenty-seven-year-old third-generation Puerto Rican who identifies racially as human, gives the benefit of the doubt rather than accusing the United States of intentionally appropriating the term "American":

The whole Western Hemisphere is American, right? It's North and South America. So anybody on the North and South American continents is American. The thing about the United States, though, is that since the United States was the first country to get their independence, the people within the United States are considered "the Americans." I don't think it is necessarily the Americans' fault, or the United States citizens' fault. It was just that the United States was a country that came to world power, and it was the greatest world power in the Western Hemisphere, and for a long time for the rest of the world. So, they represented the Western Hemisphere. They represented the Americas. That's why they're called the Americans. I don't think at any point in the United States history they said, "Look, we're the Americans and they are not," necessarily. I think now people view it that way, and I think the rest of the world views the

United States as the Americans because of the statement that they made throughout history.

For Michael, the designation of the term "American" as a U.S. national identity is more of a historical accident than an intentional appropriation. He believes that Mexicans and Canadians also "deserve the name American just like people from the United States do. I don't think the people of the United States really did anything more than anybody else to deserve specifically just them the term 'American.' We're all Americans because we're all in a continent of America." Yet he hesitates to call himself American because "I don't know where I fit. It's a question I've been asking myself. But if I had to choose an answer, I'd say I'm an American because I was born in an American continent. I'm not an American because I was born in the United States." Not fitting into the American ethnoracial ideal, Michael then subscribes to a more intercontinental meaning of American rather than to the national definition.

Whereas Michael gives the United States the benefit of the doubt, many other Latino millennials are less forgiving and plainly say that the United States appropriated the term "American." Giving a historical lesson, Raúl, who had previously paired American with the ethnoracial ideal, goes on to explain how the United States usurped the term "American" for national identity:

Well, American is just someone who's born within this country which is called America which was, you know, illegally constructed and established by British men. And it was named after Amerigo Vespucci, which people have thought the he was the first explorer here. Explorer, again, in quotes, but actually intruder. And they named it after him. From there on, I think by considering oneself American, or—yes, it's a nationality, but it is also, considering the indigenous people who live here, it's almost an insult and an affront to their history within this land, because it was a term that was made by Caucasian, by white people, and you know, it was just named America. It completely disregarded other people who were living here. And so that is almost like sanctioning the theft of this land, its resources and subjugation of the indigenous people who are here. So I think that's the real historical and social consequences that I guess the term "American" can be.

For Raúl, the United States not only illegally stole the land from the indigenous inhabitants but also misappropriated the term "American."

A few youths say that they refuse to use the term "American" to define people from the United States and instead propose what they believe are more suitable terms. Dolores, a twenty-eight-year-old fourth-generation Mexican who identifies racially as Hispanic white, says that she uses the expression "from the United States" rather than "American":

> I've struggled with that term for a while and I feel like, I don't like when it's used, I don't know what other term could be used. In Spanish we have more options because you can say, you know, from the United States, rather than American. Because I strictly like to use that term [from the United States] because "American" can refer to anybody from Mexico, Central America, South America. Even Canada if you want to. So I think it refers to a continent and to the whole Western Hemisphere almost, you know. So I feel like, I don't generally use that term. . . . If I defined it, American is . . . somebody from the United States even though I rather not use it because I don't like that it can be seen as disrespectful to other people who are from South America, Central America. I guess somebody from the United States, I would just, you have to be very careful with that term and I tend to rarely use it.

Although Dolores recognizes that "American" is used colloquially to refer to U.S. national identity, she avoids using it because it represents a slight to other North, Central, and South Americans.

Two other youths made up new labels to refer to people from the United States. For instance, Carlos, a twenty-four-year-old second-generation Mexican Guatemalan who identifies his race as white, came up with the term "USAnian." He explains, "To me personally, it would be someone who comes from any of the Americas, really. I mean, I know what people are trying to say when they say 'American,' but ever since I was little, I always pictured it like that. Ever since my senior year of high school, if I wanted to identify someone from the United States I would say 'USAnian,' you know? And yes, it included me . . . so, if you want to relate it more to the social side, to me it is people who are here in the United States." Because he believes this use of "American" to be a misappropriation, Carlos prefers to use an intercontinental definition of "American" and designate people from the United States by other terms—such as "USAnian." Providing a more scathing critique of the appropriation of the term "American" by the United States, Cathy, a twenty-year-old second-generation Mexican who identifies her race as human, favors the term "United Statesian." As she explains:

> The term "American" is an egotistical claim to nationalism by United States citizens. . . . America stretches from the northernmost point in Canada to the southernmost point of Chile. That's why the areas are *North, Central, and South America.* Anyone that lives within those borders is *American.* This is because the United States does not have a name. Consider that Mexico is actually the United States of the Mexican Republic. China is the Republic of China. . . . The United States of America is simply a statement. That's why earlier I said I'm Mexican United Statesian. I know it doesn't have the same ring to it, but maybe this country should get a name. . . . By the way, I'm also in the process of acquiring double citizenship with Mexico; therefore, I'll be twice as American as people that were simply born in the U.S.

For Cathy, the adoption of American as a national identity is an intentional misappropriation by the United States. She argues that U.S. nationals should be called "United Statesian." That she is a U.S. national of Mexican descent who has the intention of seeking Mexican citizenship makes her more American than people who are just born in the United States. Other Latino millennials shared this sense that their Latin American ancestry makes them more American than people who cannot trace their ancestry to the Americas.

Realizing that others view the designation of U.S. nationals as Americans as an illegitimate appropriation, Orlando, a twenty-two-year-old second-generation Mexican who identifies racially as white, infuses his answers with historical facts. His narrative shows the shifting meaning of "American" when these youths encounter challenging discourses:

> When I hear the term "American," I think of pretty much—when I was young, I thought of a white person. But as I grew older, I considered myself American, Mexican American, as American pertains to someone or a citizen living in the United States. But when I went abroad, I mentioned

America. I went to Venezuela. They considered themselves American. Living on the American continent, which I never thought of it that way. They started referring to me as a North American, which is kind of weird. When I mentioned America down there, they're all [like], "Oh, you're talking about us as well." It was weird. I never thought about it that way, America [not as in] North America, but as in North, South, Central. Even still to this day, I can't catch on to that. I feel that an American is someone living in the United States.

Orlando's narrative shows that the meaning of American shifts over time and across settings. As a child he held to an ethnoracial definition of American that, as he aged, shifted to birthright. New experiences, such as travel abroad, brings these millennials face-to-face with others who contest the U.S. appropriation of the term "American." Whereas youths like Carlos and Cathy have developed a critical stance toward the term, Orlando, although he is aware of these critiques, ultimately claims a more colloquial definition of "American" based on being a U.S. national, perhaps as a way to fit in the American imagined community.

Developing an Integrated Subjectivity

At the beginning of this chapter, Manuel states without hesitation that he is a citizen but that being an American is "up for discussion." In his ensuing narrative, Manuel sheds light on why he says this, beginning by explaining that he had a "traditional" American childhood filled with music, sports, and holidays and "doing American kid things." According to Manuel, "I grew up listening to punk rock, rock and roll and drinking PBR. Like, you know what I mean? Like doing American kid things. Like football and playing pee wee baseball. So I think in that traditional sense. Fourth of July barbeques." Yet he acknowledges that his was not the typical American childhood as his family blended American with Mexican traditions:

Definitely, but it's not in that rigid like mold that we have of Americans. It's like, for example, we had Thanksgiving at my mom's house. My parents had turkey. We had ham, yams. We had mashed potatoes, gravy. Like that's something you consider typical United States of America food. You know? But then for Christmas we had tamales, pozole, and like all these Mexican foods. So there's instances where we'll have barbeque and it is hot dogs and brats and burgers, and then another one where there's carne asada [steak] and goat meat. I guess it's a combination of both so it's my own Americanism.

This blending of cultures leads to what Manuel calls his "own Americanism." He adds that "in this country it's like you need an interpreter. You're not WASP so it's like this in-between. It's like I'm not Mexican [but] I'm not complete[ly] American so it's like I said I'm this multicultural. Like hybrid, you know, with two cultures." Manuel sees himself as a "hybrid" because he is made of two cultures, and it is this combination that makes his "own Americanism," that is, his own brand of American. He does not see himself as an American in the conventional way, at least "not in that rigid like mold that we have of Americans." He is a different kind of American, but an American nevertheless.

Like Manuel, Latino millennials point to their "ethnic" upbringing at home while being socialized as "Americans" via growing up in the United States. That is, these youths see themselves as both American and ethnic, and to them, there is no conflict between these identities. They think of themselves are neither *just* American nor *just* ethnic but as both simultaneously. Thus, their own form of Americanism, as Manuel calls it, involves both identities—a blend of American and Latin American cultures. In other words, these youths develop what Benmayor (2002) calls an *integrated subjectivity* that brings together both cultures and results in an American national identity that coexists with their ethnic identification. As Jessica, a twenty-four-year-old second-generation woman who identifies racially as Mexican, succinctly puts it, "Well I'm Mexican, but I'm also an American." I found that an integrated subjectivity was widespread among the Latino millennials in the study and that there were no discernible factors (such as gender, educational level, racial identification, or form of contestation) linked to the development of an integrated subjectivity. Regardless of the form of contestation these youths engaged in, they were all likely to form an integrated subjectivity.

For Latino millennials, being American and being ethnic are separate identities that complement and exist alongside each other: American is their national identity, while their specific national group is their ethnic identity. Edwin, a twenty-eight-year-old second-generation Mexican who identifies racially as Hispanic, explains that being American "means that you were born in this country. I'm Mexican, but I'm American too because I was born here. But I don't consider American an ethnicity. That's why I say I'm Mexican. . . . Well, I'm American because I was born here. I am legal, but I'm still Mexican." As Edwin states, American is his national identity derived from his U.S. birth, while Mexican is his ethnic identity that comes from his family's origin. This feeling of duality is exemplified by Cynthia, a twenty-year-old second-generation Mexican who refused to answer the race questions, when she states that her parents are "Mexican because they grew up there. . . . I guess I'm Mexican through them, but I'm also American because I literally grew up here and it's my country, my home."

Growing up with both cultures allows these youths to develop what Silvestrini (1997) calls a *fluid sense of self* that permits movement between these two worlds. Laura's earlier statement about the United States as the land of opportunity can be seen in a new light when she says that her family incorporated American and Mexican cultures into their family traditions. She explains, "My family did adopt like the Fourth of July, you know, we don't celebrate that in Mexico, but we do like celebrate holidays that they typically don't in Mexico. So we intertwine them because we know we live here and need to immerse ourselves in the culture. So, I mean, my parents are U.S. citizens, but I consider them as separate, but because we live here. We all are American because we live here and have to celebrate their culture as well—so it's our culture." Although her parents remain Mexicans despite their U.S. citizenship, Laura and her siblings see both cultures as their own. Like Laura, many of these youths are bicultural, easily shifting between one culture and the other.

Some youths use the term "Mexican American" to denote this duality. Danny follows his earlier critique of "wannabe-white" Latinos by stating that he considers himself American, but he quickly interjects that he is Mexican American "mainly because I can relate to both places. I was born and raised here, but my parents grew up over there, so I know their culture, but I also know this culture." Leo, a twenty-six-year-old second-generation Mexican who identifies as Latino, also uses "Mexican American" to stress this duality when saying "I am Mexican American, though. I am in touch with my American side and my Mexican side." Despite being Puerto Rican, Mariely, a twenty-three-year-old third-generation woman who identifies racially as Hispanic, also uses terms like "Mexican American" to convey Americanization:

> You have embraced the culture of this country which is a white culture but still maintain a little bit of your own culture. Like Mexican American. . . . You adapted to the country you live in, becoming quote unquote Americanized. Every legal citizen of this country is an American. How can you not embrace the culture if you live here! You have adapted one way or another. Either through school or education or language or something. Well, I was born here. So I know nothing but the American culture. But I also know a little about my Puerto Rican traditions too.

As Mariely points out, it is impossible for Latino millennials to not also be American because of their upbringing in the United States.

It is also inconceivable for Latino millennials to stop identifying with their families' ethnic backgrounds despite growing up in the United States. Niurka, a twenty-two-year-old second-generation Dominican who identifies racially as Latina, says, "I'm definitely an American. I'm proud to be here, but I'm also Dominican and will not forget that." This sentiment is shared by Heriberto, a twenty-year-old second-generation man who identifies ethnically as Hispanic and racially as Mexican, when he states, "I am an American because I was born here. . . . I believe that I am an American and always will be, but I never want to let go of my Mexican heritage because although I was not born there, it is a huge part of who I am." Although these youths are both American and ethnic, their strongest attachment is to their ethnicity. This sentiment is echoed by Giselle, a twenty-three-year-old second-generation Mexican who identifies racially as other, Hispanic, and Latina. Giselle exclaims, "I am not fully American. I mean, I know I consider myself Mexican American. I speak the English language. I comply with values and laws of the country and the state where I live in. With regard to attachment or, having some bond with, I can't say I have a, a strong bond [to being American]." Like Giselle, these youths are American but they do not feel as connected to that identity. Their ethnic bond is so strong that leaving behind their ethnic identification is nonnegotiable. These youths insist in their "own kind of Americanism"—and that is one that includes their ethnicity. Dolores revisits her previous question on the suitability of the term "American" for people like her when she gives her own version of an integrated subjectivity:

> You asked me how I fit into that idea of American? . . . I fit into it as long as I can maintain my ethnic identity with it, hand in hand at the same time and not ascribe to a very limited homogeneous white idea of what being American means. So as long as I can continue to embrace who I am ethnically and culturally, then I feel like I can fit into American. But the minute it begins to exclude or it creates an idea of who that can include, then I don't identify with it.

Dolores sees herself as an American when the term's definition is not limited to the ethnoracial ideal.

Because these identities are intertwined, it is hard for these youths to fathom being just American or just Mexican. Julia, a seventeen-year-old second-generation woman who identifies racially as Mexican, hangs on to her ethnicity and is baffled by "people that just completely lose their native language and just become American, and it strikes me as odd." Rather than selecting one or the other, these youths typically pick and choose what makes them American and what makes them ethnic. Yuli, a twenty-three-year-old Mexican who identifies racially as Hispanic, prefers to identify as Mexican but recognizes that there is "a lot of American in me." Yuli says, "I think that even though I choose to identify myself as solely Mexican, I have a lot of American in me [laughs]. Just based on certain things that I've picked up from the American culture, such as the whole independent thing. Being independent from my family, which is highly frowned upon. I don't know, I definitely think that I've picked up some of the American culture but . . . I've generally been picking and choosing from both cultures, which is sometimes problematic but sometimes not." Having two cultures gives Yuli the option of adopting aspects of both cultures.

It is also difficult for these youths to come to terms with their American side. Priscilla, a twenty-six-year-old second-generation woman who identifies racially as Mexican, only accepted her Americanness once she realized that being Mexican does not make her any less American. Priscilla explains, "I have had a lot of battles with that because only a year ago I accepted the American part of my ethnicity, so to be American it means to live here, to grow up here, to have the experiences that any other person that lives in this country could have. Mine has been slightly different because I have had the Mexican culture and traditions, a part of it, but that doesn't make me any less American." Again, Danny expresses his struggle to reconcile his American and his Mexican identities because they are connected to different spaces and places. He says, "I guess I'm Mexican American. I am torn between being American and being Mexican. . . . I consider myself Mexican, but I'm still American. I partially belong in certain places of the United States and certain places in Mexico. . . . Well, certain neighborhoods like Pilsen and Mexican neighborhoods are more accepting. . . . Well, because I'm Mexican, I don't fit in. They don't see me as part of the country." Although in general Danny does not feel accepted, he finds solace in Mexican neighborhoods where he feels that he fits in and where his own type of Americanism is recognized and validated.

Constructing Their Own Americanism

My analysis suggests that rather than civic nationalism, the United States is characterized by ethnoracial nationalism, in which race and/or culture determines who belongs. Despite the inclusive rhetoric, it is only those who are white, of European descent, and Christian who are uncontestably American, while the Americanness of those who do not meet the ethnoracial criteria is contested. Latino millennials' narratives show that their apparent disconnection from the American national identity—reflected in their frequent reluctance to define themselves as "real" Americans—is a direct response to their ethnoracial exclusion from the American imaginary and is not based on the rejection of American values. Growing up in the United States, these youths have adopted American ideals, yet they cannot meet the ethnoracial criteria because of their physical and/or cultural traits. It is this inability to meet the racial and/or cultural criteria that stands in the way of being seen by others—and of seeing themselves—as rightfully American.

In addition to their hesitation to identify as Americans, my analysis shows that Latino millennials actively—and often vigorously—contest the othering that negates their Americanness. They do so by stressing the ways in which they too are American—and often more American than those doubting them. I found that gender, education, and racial identification were the only intervening factors determining the type of contestation that Latino millennials engaged in. While gender and education seem to have a slight effect, racial identification largely shaped the form of contestation that these youths followed. I also found that regardless of their gender, educational level, and racial identification, these youths were equally likely to develop a sense of themselves as Americans that incorporated their dual subjectivity as Latinos and Americans.

By engaging in claims of ethnoracial citizenship, these youths develop notions of belonging that challenge the dominant ethnoracial ideology and allow them to locate themselves as authentic members of the American national community. To do so, they employ familiar American tropes that emphasize how similar they are to fellow Americans. They also deploy tropes that highlight the various ways in which they think they are *more* American than those who fit the dominant ethnoracial criteria. It is through the use of these familiar tropes that they offer a counternarrative that not only challenges dominant notions of belonging but also voices their demand for inclusion. They contest the white, Anglo-Saxon, Protestant, heteronormative, and male ethnoracial foundation of the national identity, push for a more inclusive society, and insert themselves as legitimate members of American society (Flores and Benmayor 1997). They develop an integrated subjectivity and gain a "fluid sense of self" that allows them to move—although not as easily—between their multiple worlds while staking their claims to both (see Silvestrini 1997). Pushing for their own Americanism—that is, setting their own terms for becoming American—creates a crack at the door, one that they will continue to pick at in their demand for inclusion in the American national imaginary.

6

Rethinking Race and Belonging among Latino Millennials

I began to conceptualize this book in the midst of a storm of racist social media comments spurred by the performance of "The Star-Spangled Banner" and "God Bless America" by Latino singers Sebastien De La Cruz and Marc Anthony at two separate professional sporting events. The fact that each of these singers is a U.S.-born citizen did not prevent the launching of racist and xenophobic epithets such as "foreigner," "illegal alien," "beaner," and "spic." Social media commentators described the singers as non-American and thus unfit to perform such patriotic songs. Twitter posts made no distinction between Mexicans and Puerto Ricans, or citizens and undocumented immigrants. Sebastien De La Cruz was again bashed on social media—this time for singing the national anthem at a Democratic Party presidential debate. To these public reactions are added those expressed by Donald Trump, who, running on an explicitly nativist platform, was elected as U.S. president on the Republican ticket. On the campaign trail, Trump used familiar tropes of crime, drug smuggling, "illegal" immigration, rape, and infectious disease to pounce on Mexicans and, by extension, all Latinos. He also called into question the integrity of U.S. district judge Gonzalo Curiel because his Mexican ancestry, and presumed pro-immigrant stance, made him unfit to preside on a case against Trump University. Trump vowed to eliminate the birthright citizenship of so-called anchor babies—a pejorative term for U.S.-born children of undocumented immigrants—and to build a wall on the U.S.-Mexico border to stop the "illegal" flow of Mexicans. These tropes are part of what Chavez (2013) calls the "Latino threat narrative."

Trump's inflammatory and racist rhetoric is worrisome for Latinos. Young Latinos—including children, teenagers, and young adults—are concerned about what will happen to them under Trump's presidency. Despite being U.S. citizens by birth, they wonder if they will be deported or physically harmed. These fears are legitimate, as the day after the election, there were reports of verbal and physical violence against Latinos and other groups that Trump had targeted during his campaign. More worrisome for these youths is the escalation of detention and deportation of undocumented immigrants who do not have a criminal record. These youths are aware that—just like Sebastien De La Cruz and Marc Anthony—they signify "illegal" and "Mexican" regardless of their actual legal status and national origin. The pervasiveness of these nativist expressions, and the realization that half of the electorate voted for president someone who espouses such views conveys to these young Latinos that they do not belong. These expressions also poignantly show that U.S. citizenship does not wholly protect individuals of Latin American descent from having their Americanness questioned or stripped. Within this context of anti-Latino rhetoric, this new generation of Latinos is developing notions about their place in the American national landscape and as I show in this book, many are challenging these nativist notions and claiming their rightful place as Americans.

The narratives presented in this book show that vitriolic racist and nativist discourses—such as those in social media and in Donald Trump's speeches—are far from exceptional. Combined with more subtle racial microaggressions, anti-Latino rhetoric is a reality experienced by Latino millennials day in and out. New forms of racism in the post–civil rights era mar the daily lives of Latinos and shape their sense of identity and social positioning. Their stories attest to the persistence of spatial segregation despite efforts to dismantle it. They narrate how their presence in white places and spaces often elicits reactions that peel away their sense of belonging and leave them excluded from the American imagined community.

In this book, I have shown that these youths' exclusion has birthed three interrelated subjectivities—Latinos as an ethnorace, a racial middle, and "real" Americans. These subjectivities underscore Latino millennials' reactions to their lack of a meaningful racial category, an appropriate place in the racial hierarchy, and acceptance as co-nationals, respectively. Using a social constructionist framework, the preceding pages have examined how Latino millennials form these self-understandings and imagine themselves as members of U.S. society. I traced how race—as it is understood and enacted in everyday life—shapes Latino millennials' notions of belonging. In this conclusion, I focus on two larger questions I have engaged throughout: *How do La-*

tinos understand their place in the U.S. racial landscape? And what does the Latino experience tell us about current developments in the U.S. racial landscape? While the former contributes to the long-standing question of Latinos' fit into the larger American community, the latter furthers our theoretical understandings of belonging in U.S. society.

Reframing the Theoretical Discourses on Latinos

One of the issues I address in this book revolves around Latinos' self-understandings of their ethnoracial categorization, position, and status in U.S. society. By unraveling their narratives, I shed light on how they identify racially, where they locate themselves in the racial hierarchy, and how they understand themselves as Americans. The other issue that I address in this book concerns scholarly formulations about Latinos' place in the American national landscape. I contend that traditional theoretical frameworks fall short when applied to Latinos, and that we would be better served by a theoretical overhaul that could more accurately position Latinos within the American imaginary. In particular, I critique three established theoretical frameworks that in their current iterations cannot adequately account for the ways in which Latino millennials understand themselves.

One of my main findings is that Latino millennials reject standard racial categories and favor ethnic and panethnic labels. Rather than identifying racially as white or black—standard categories that they feel do not reflect their experiences and cultural backgrounds—these youths inserted ethnic and panethnic designations as stand-ins for race. Specifically, they applied "Latino," "Hispanic," and national origin labels in response to queries about their racial identification. These alternative ways of identifying align with the "Some Other Race" category used in the U.S. Census. These youths' narratives underscore the inadequacy of current racial options for people who have undergone a particular form of racialization and are identifiable physically or culturally as part of a separate social group. As their narratives show, these youths see themselves and are seen by others as part of a distinct "social origin" or ethnoracial group composed of people of Latin American origin.

Based on my analysis, I contend that Latino millennials' racial identification poses a challenge to our current theorization about race in the

United States. What Dowling (2014) calls the "question of race" among Latinos points to the inconsistencies that characterize Latino racial identification (what people say they are when they fill out forms) and racial identity (what people actually believe they are). At the center of this polemic is the sizable number of Latinos who—like the millennials in this study—are dissatisfied with the existing racial categories and opt out of them by marking SOR. My data expose the faulty assumption that racial identification matches racial identity and suggest that racial identification is often based on choosing the least ill-fitting category. Underlying the "question of race" and racial mismatch among Latinos is our flawed conceptualization of race and ethnicity as separate identity concepts. My analysis suggests that ethnorace may be a more fitting concept with which to tackle the question of race among Latinos. Rather than splitting race and ethnicity conceptually, ethnorace merges these concepts and accounts for the roles that both race and ethnicity play in how Latinos form self-understandings that allow them to negotiate their position in the U.S. racial landscape.

My second major finding shows that these youths locate themselves in a unique and separate position in the U.S. racial structure. By and large, these youths conceive of a racial order structured by a color line with whites at the top and blacks at the bottom. A few acquiesced to the black and white racial divide by placing themselves on either side of the color line, while some refused to play the game altogether by rejecting the racial structure and refusing to specify a racial location. However, the vast majority of the Latino millennials placed themselves in an intermediate position in the racial hierarchy. These youths proclaimed that they were "in the middle," or "in between" whites and blacks. That is, they thought of themselves as occupying a "racial middle."

My analysis challenges current notions of the U.S. racial structure and color line. Similar to the inaccuracy of substituting racial identification for racial identity, it may be erroneous to use Latinos' racial identification as a proxy for racial location. Yet dominant discourses about the U.S. racial structure do exactly that, building up to a faulty understanding of the U.S. racial order and the position of Latinos in it. And while triracial models—which posit Latinos as a racial middle—identify the complexities of racial positioning in the United States, the racial middle remains undertheorized. Building on Kim's (1999) racial triangulation model, I have teased out the "racial middle" and shown that, rather than a single catchall category, there are different middles that reflect unique patterns of racialization along multiple dimensions. By claiming the racial middle, Latino millennials vie for inclusion in the U.S. racial structure.

My third main finding is that Latino millennials were reluctant to identify as Americans. Their hesitation reflects a sense of not being "real Americans" or being just a "different kind of American." These youths' narratives show that their disconnect from a national U.S. identity is a reaction to their inability to meet its ethnoracial criteria. They are aware that "American" signifies white Anglo-Saxon Protestant and that they do not meet this standard. Against this, they make claims to a national identity by emphasizing their subscription to other "American" tropes, such as freedom, opportunity, patriotism, and multiculturalism. As such, they embrace a vision of civil nationalism in order to insert themselves into the national imaginary and create a new vision of what it means to be an American.

Based on my analysis, I expand on Rosaldo's (1997) Latino cultural citizenship framework. Although I find this framework useful, its emphasis on cultural difference as the leading source of exclusion overlooks the significant role that race plays in Latino exclusion from national identity. Its corollary, Tsuda's (2014) racial citizenship framework, downplays culture while focusing on the impact of racial traits on exclusion from national identity. Based on my findings, I propose a hybrid framework— which I have labeled *ethnoracial citizenship*—to account for the cultural and racial dimensions that shape how Latinos are defined as outsiders of the national community and how they deploy counternarratives to stake claims of belonging. In claiming their Americanness, these youths deploy a counternarrative based on familiar American tropes that let them define themselves as authentic Americans.

Latinos, Intersectionality, and Race Theorizing

Drawing on an intersectional approach, I looked for any signs of interaction effects. By deliberately making connections between social categorizations such as gender, skin color, phenotype, class, and ethnicity, it became clear that certain combinations resulted in increased frequency, intensity, and forms of discrimination. Those who exhibited any of the characteristics prone to elicit discrimination—such as being a male, darker-skinned, phenotypically Latino, low-income, or a Spanish speaker—had increased chances of experiencing discrimination, but when two or three of these characteristics combined, their odds magnified. As a result, not all Latinos were affected by discrimination equally.

Although clear patterns emerged in the analysis that underscore the effect of the intersecting social categorizations, I also found that among Latinos interactional differences are a matter of degree rather than of kind. Ultimately, the frequency, intensity, and type of racial experiences may fluctuate according to a person's characteristics, but the underlying racial experiences remain largely consistent for all Latino millennials in this study. Despite individual characteristics that may tone down negative racial experiences, no Latino is completely immune to discrimination. An intersectional approach therefore helps us better understand why Latinos with different social characteristics often hold similar self-understandings. My analysis shows that Latino millennials experience discrimination regardless of their characteristics, but that the frequency, intensity, and type of racial experiences vary. Those who were darker-skinned tend to experience more frequent and intense discrimination, which escalates if they are males and further increases among those of lower socioeconomic status or those who speak Spanish in public. We could then think of lighter skin color, female gender, higher social class, and unaccented English as "protective factors" that mitigate the frequency and intensity of certain types of discrimination but that do not completely eliminate it. As I uncovered, Latin American ancestry weighs heavily on Latino millennials' racialization as minorities and immigrants, regardless of the absence of visible markers. An intersectional approach, then, provides a more complex lens for understanding how these youths see themselves in relation to the racial and national landscape. Future research should more deeply explore other forms of intersectionality that may affect Latino millennials' self-understandings.

Latino Millennials Matter

The Latino millennials whose narratives are presented in this book conveyed the day-to-day racial experiences that erode their sense of belonging. Their stories tell of their struggle to reconcile their legitimate status as Americans with the messages—in words and practices—they receive every day that strip them of their Americanness. What will result from the constant suspicion they face? And what effect will their accompanying feelings of estrangement have on the social, economic, and political life of this country? How will their experiences shape how they engage as citizens?

It would be easy to disregard the stories told by Latino millennials as developmental flukes prompted by their search for identity, or by the wave of Latino immigrant activism preceding the interviews. It is plausible that as they reach midadulthood, their views will temper. But with the current escalation of anti-immigrant sentiment—which is particularly directed at Mexicans—it is unlikely that Latino millennials' sense of estrangement from the national community will subside. In the current political context, escalation of this sentiment looms as nativism plays out in President Trump's incendiary talk. The following narrative from Diego, a twenty-two-year-old second-generation Mexican, is more relevant today than it was when he told it in 2009:

> You're expected to assimilate, and if you don't, then you're outcasted. And I think that reflects a lot of this wave of xenophobia that we have in this country right now. Because a lot of people don't want to let go of their roots. Don't want to let go of their culture. Don't want to speak English. They don't want to completely assimilate, they want to hang on to what they know, their traditions, their customs. . . . I would say English is important, but I don't think that it should be so black and white. Either you learn it and you become a citizen or you're able to become part of this country or society, or you don't and you stay an outcast, in the shadows. I don't think it should be like that. . . . Maybe I'm not too American citizen oriented [long silence]. The first thing that popped into my mind [when thinking who is a citizen] was holding an American flag, a white man holding an American flag screaming at me. Not sure why. Maybe to be conservative, to be a Minuteman. To be xenophobic, to be against any foreigner. . . . I mean, legally, technically, yes [I am a citizen]. But, I don't really feel like a citizen. . . . I don't really feel like integrated. I don't feel proud to be living in this country. I don't rep it. I won't hold an American flag, unless it's upside down. I'm serious, I won't. And in a lot of the

[immigrant rights] marches, a lot of the protests, a lot of people try to give me flags, "Oh, here. Hold this. Here you go." I just can't do it. I don't know if that's because I'm anti-American, you know, someone would label me anti-American, whatever. I think it's—in order for me to really be an American citizen and be proud of being one, I would want to feel right, you know what I'm saying? I would want to feel like I have rights in this country. . . . I feel like a lot of them are deprived or taken away at the snap of a finger. I feel like they can be bent too. You have the right to remain silent. You know? It don't even work like that sometimes, you don't even have rights a lot of times . . . [so] I'm not, I don't think I am. I don't feel like a citizen. If anything, I can relate more to the undocumented population than I can to the citizens. Maybe that's because racially . . . it's kind of like an ideology, like us versus them. You know, the Americans versus the undocumented or the illegals or the Mexicans. Maybe that, by default, that places me on the other side. Or that places me on one side, so it's kind of like a battle . . . because a lot of this, a lot of this hate is because people from the third world, people from Latin America, they're not considered citizens, they're considered illegal aliens, you know. So, yeah, that's what it is, you know what I'm saying? Illegal aliens versus citizens.

In this riveting account, Diego narrates the internal struggle that Latino millennials wage daily in trying to reconcile what it means to be an American of Latin American ancestry. As I read over his words, I am transported to broad images of Donald Trump's rallies and to his inflammatory rhetoric that cast Latinos, regardless of citizenship status, as people who do not belong and who should be tossed out of the country. Diego masterfully shows how this nation's narrative cheats Latinos out of a sense of national belonging, even though they are Americans. Like Diego and the millennials I write about, today's youths are aiming to rewrite the national narrative on belonging—one in which American is inclusive of racial and ethnic diversity.

REFERENCES

Abrego, Leisy. 2014. *Sacrificing Families: Navigating Laws, Labor, and Love across Borders*. Palo Alto, CA: Stanford University Press.

Alcoff, Linda Martin. 2006. *Visible Identities: Race, Gender, and the Self*. New York: Oxford University Press.

———. 2009. "Latinos beyond the Binary." *Southern Journal of Philosophy* 47 (S1): 112–28.

Almaguer, Tomas. 2008. *Racial Fault Lines: The Historical Origins of White Supremacy in California*. Berkeley: University of California Press.

Almaguer, Tomas, and Moon-Kie Jung. 1998. "The Enduring Ambiguities of Race in the United States." Center for Research on Social Organization Working Paper Series, University of Michigan.

Anderson, Benedict. 2006. *Imagined Communities: Reflections on the Origin and Spread of Nationalism*. 3rd ed. New York: Verso.

Anderson, Elijah. 2015. "The White Space." *Sociology of Race and Ethnicity* 1:10–21.

Aparicio, Frances. 2016. "Not Fully Boricuas: Puerto Rican Intralatino/as in Chicago." *CENTRO: Journal of the Center for Puerto Rican Studies* 28 (3): 154–79.

Barreto, Matt, and Gary Segura. 2014. *Latino America: How America's Most Dynamic Population Is Poised to Transform the Politics of the Nation*. San Francisco: Public Press.

Beltran, Cristina. 2010. *The Trouble with Unity: Latino Politics and the Creation of Identity*. New York: Oxford University Press.

Benmayor, Rina. 2002. "Narrating Cultural Citizenship: Oral Histories of Latina/o First-Generation College Students." *Social Justice* 29 (4): 90–121.

Bennett, Sue, Karl Maton, and Lisa Kervin. 2008. "The 'Digital Natives' Debate: A Critical Review of the Evidence." *British Journal of Educational Technology* 39 (5): 775–86.

Bloemraad, Irene. 2013. "Being American/Becoming American: Birthright Citizenship and Immigrants' Membership in the United States." *Studies in Law, Politics and Society* 60:55–84.

Bobo, Lawrence D., and Ryan A. Smith. 1998. "From Jim Crow Racism to Laissez-Faire Racism: The Transformation of Racial Attitudes." In *Beyond Pluralism: The Conception of Groups and Group Identities in America.*, edited by Wendy F. Katkin, Ned Landsman, and Andrea Tyree, 182–220. Urbana: University of Illinois Press.

Bonilla-Silva, Eduardo. 2003. "New Racism: Color-Blind Racism, and the Future of Whiteness in America." In *White Out: The Continuing Significance of Racism*, edited by Ashley W. Doane and Eduardo Bonilla-Silva, 271–84. New York: Taylor and Francis.

———. 2004. "From Bi-racial to Tri-racial: Towards a New System of Racial Stratification in the USA." *Ethnic and Racial Studies* 27 (6): 931–50.

———. 2013. *Racism without Racists: Color-Blind Racism and the Persistence of Racial Inequality in America*. 4th ed. Lanham, MD: Rowman and Littlefield.

Brown, Anna, and Mark Hugo Lopez. 2013. *Mapping the Latino Population, by State, County and City*. Washington, DC: Pew Hispanic Center, August. www.pewhispanic.org.

Calderon, José. 1992. "Hispanic and Latino: The Viability of Categories for Panethnic Unity." *Latin American Perspectives* 19 (4): 37–44.

Campbell, Mary E., and Christabel L. Rogalin. 2006. "Categorical Imperatives: The Interaction of Latino and Racial Identification." *Social Science Quarterly* 87 (5): 1030–52.

Carbado, Devon. 2005. "Racial Naturalization." *American Quarterly* 57:633–58.

Castles, Stephen, and Alastair Davidson. 2000. *Citizenship and Migration*. New York: Routledge.

Chapa, Jorge. 2000. "Hispanic/Latino Ethnicity and Identifiers." In *Encyclopedia of the U.S. Census*, edited by Rolf Anderson. Washington, DC: Congressional Quarterly Press.

Chavez, Leo. 2013. *The Latino Threat: Constructing Immigrants, Citizens, and the Nation*. 2nd ed. Palo Alto, CA: Stanford University Press.

Chicago Metropolitan Agency for Planning. 2011. *Latino Population Growth Drives Metropolitan Chicago's Population Growth*. www.cmap.illinois.gov.

Cornell, Stephen E., and Douglas Hartmann. 1998. *Ethnicity and Race: Making Identities in a Changing World*. 2nd ed. Thousand Oaks, CA: Sage.

Dávila, Arlene. 2001. *Latinos Inc.: Marketing and the Making of a People*. Berkeley: University of California Press.

———. 2008. *Latino Spin: Public Image and the Whitewashing of Race*. New York: New York University Press.

DeGenova, Nicholas. 2005. *Working the Boundaries: Race, Space, and "Illegality" in Mexican Chicago*. Durham, NC: Duke University Press.

DeGenova, Nicholas, and Ana Yolanda Ramos-Zayas. 2003. *Latino Crossings: Mexicans, Puerto Ricans, and the Politics of Race and Citizenship*. New York: Taylor and Francis.

DeSipio, Louis. 1996. "More Than the Sum of Its Parts: The Building Blocks of a Pan-Ethnic Latino Identity." In *The Politics of Minority Coalitions: Race, Ethnicity and Shared Uncertainties*, edited by Rich Wilbur, 177–89. Westport, CT: Praeger.

Desmond, Matthew, and Mustafa Emirbayer. 2009. "What Is Racial Domination?" *Du Bois Review: Social Science Research on Race* 6 (2): 335–55.

Dovidio, John F., and Samuel L. Gaertner. 1996. "Affirmative Action, Unintentional Racial Biases, and Intergroup Relations." *Journal of Social Issues* 52 (4): 51–75.

Dowling, Julie. 2014. *Mexican Americans and the Race Question*. Austin: University of Texas Press.

Duany, Jorge. 2002. *The Puerto Rican Nation on the Move: Identities on the Island and in the United States*. Chapel Hill: University of North Carolina Press.

Dungy, Gwendolyn Jordan. 2011. "A National Perspective: Testing Our Assumptions about Generation Cohorts." In *Diverse Millennial Students in College: Implications for Faculty and Student Affairs*, edited by Fred Bonner II, Aretha F. Marbley, and Mary F. Howard Hamilton, 5–21. Sterling, VA: Stylus.

Eschbach, Karl, and Christina Gomez. 1998. "Choosing Hispanic Identity: Ethnic Identity Switching among Respondents in High School and Beyond." *Social Science Quarterly* 79 (1): 74–90.

Essed, Philomena. 1991. *Understanding Everyday Racism*. Newbury Park, CA: Sage.

Feagin, Joe. 2013. *Systemic Racism: A Theory of Oppression*. New York: Routledge.

Feagin, Joe R., and Jose A. Cobas. 2014. *Latinos Facing Racism: Discrimination, Resistance, and Endurance*. Boulder, CO: Paradigm.

Fernandez, Lilia. 2012. *Brown in the Windy City: Mexicans and Puerto Ricans in Postwar Chicago*. Chicago: University of Chicago Press.

Flores, William V. 2003. "New Citizens, New Rights: Undocumented Immigrants and Latino Cultural Citizenship." *Latin American Perspectives* 30 (2): 87–100.

Flores, William, and Rina Benmayor. 1997. "Introduction: Constructing Cultural Citizenship." In *Latino Cultural Citizenship: Claiming Identity, Space and Rights* , edited by William V. Flores and Rina Benmayor, 1–23. Boston: Beacon Press.

Flores-González, Nilda. 1999. "The Racialization of Latinos: The Meaning of Latino Identity for the Second Generation." *Latino Studies Journal* 10 (3): 3–31.

———. 2010. "Immigrants, Citizens, or Both? The Second Generation in the Immigrant Rights Marches." In *Marcha! Latino Chicago and the Immigrant Rights Movement*, edited by A. Pallares and N. Flores-González, 198–214. Urbana: University of Illinois Press.

Flores-González, Nilda, Elizabeth Aranda, and Elizabeth Vaquera. 2014. "'Doing Race': Latino Youth's Identities and the Politics of Racial Exclusion." *American Behavioral Scientist* 58:1834–51.

Flores-González, Nilda, and Michael Rodríguez-Muñíz. 2014. "Latino Solidarity, Citizenship, and Puerto Rican Youth in the Immigrant Rights Movement." In *Diaspora Studies in Education: Toward a Framework for Understanding the Experiences of Transnational Communities*, edited by Rosalie Rolón-Dow and Jason G. Irizarry, 17–38. New York: Peter Lang.

Forman, Tyrone, Carla Goar, and Amanda Lewis. 2002. "Neither Black nor White? An Empirical Test of the Latin Americanization Thesis." *Race and Society* 5:65–84.

Fox, Cybelle, and Thomas Guglielmo. 2012. "Defining America's Racial Boundaries: Blacks, Mexicans, and European Immigrants, 1890–1945." *American Journal of Sociology* 118 (2): 327–79.

Fraga, Luis, John A. Garcia, Rodney E. Hero, Michael Jones-Correa, Valerie Martinez-Ebers, and Gary M. Segura. 2010. *Latino Lives in America: Making It Home*. Philadelphia: Temple University Press, 2010.

Frank, Reanne, Ilana Redstone Akresh, and Bo Lu. 2010. "Latino Immigrants and the U.S. Racial Order: How and Where Do They Fit In?" *American Sociological Review* 75 (3): 378–401.

Frankenberg, Ruth. 1993. *White Women, Race Matters: The Social Construction of Whiteness*. Minneapolis: University of Minnesota Press.

———. 1994. "Whiteness and Americanness: Examining Constructions of Race, Culture, and Nation in White Women's Life Narratives." In *Race*, edited by Steven Gregory and Roger Sanjek, 62–77. New Brunswick, NJ: Rutgers University Press.

Gans, Herbert. 1992. "Second-Generation Decline: Scenarios for the Economic and Ethnic Futures of the Post-1965 American Immigrants." *Ethnic and Racial Studies* 15 (2): 173–92.

———. 1999. "The Possibility of a New Racial Hierarchy in the Twenty-First-Century United States." In *The Cultural Territories of Race*, edited by Michele Lamont, 371–91. Chicago: University of Chicago Press.

Garcia, Lorena, and Mérida Rúa. 2007. "Processing Latinidad: Mapping Latino Urban Landscapes through Chicago Ethnic Festivals." *Latino Studies* 5 (3): 317–39.

Golash-Boza, Tanya. 2006. "Dropping the Hyphen? Becoming Latino(a)-American through Racialized Assimilation." *Social Forces* 85:29–60.

Golash-Boza, Tanya, and William Darity Jr. 2008. "Latino Racial Choices: The Effects of Skin Colour and Discrimination on Latinos' and Latinas' Racial Self-Identifications." *Ethnic and Racial Studies* 31 (5): 899–934.

Goldberg, David Theo. 1997. *Racial Subjects: Writing on Race in America*. New York: Routledge.

Gomez, Laura E. 2007. *Manifest Destinies: The Making of the Mexican American Race*. New York: New York University Press.

Grosfoguel, Ramon. 2004. "Race and Ethnicity or Racialized Ethnicities: Identities within Global Coloniality." *Ethnicities* 4:312–37.

Gutierrez, Elena. 2008. *Fertile Matters: The Politics of Mexican-Origin Women's Reproduction*. Austin: University of Texas Press.

Guzman, Juan Carlos, Allert Brown-Gort, Andrew Deliyannides, and Roger A. Knight. 2010. *The State of Chicago: The New Equation*. Institute for Latino Studies, University of Notre Dame. latinostudies.nd.edu.

Haney Lopez, Ian. 2004. *Racism on Trial: The Chicano Fight for Justice*. Cambridge, MA: Belknap Press.

———. 2006. *White by Law: The Legal Construction of Race*. 10th anniversary edition. New York: New York University Press.

Hattam, Victoria. 2007. *In the Shadow of Race: Jews, Latinos, and Immigrant Politics in the United States*. Chicago: University of Chicago Press.

Hayes-Bautista, David E. 2004. *La Nueva California: Latinos in the Golden State*. Berkeley: University of California Press.

Hayes-Bautista, David E., and Jorge Chapa. 1987. "Latino Terminology: Conceptual Bases for Standardized Terminology." *American Journal of Public Health* 77 (1): 61–68.

Hitlin, Steven, J. Scott Brown, and Glen H. Elder Jr. 2007. "Measuring Latinos: Racial vs. Ethnic Classification and Self-Understandings." *Social Forces* 86 (2): 587–611.

Holley, Lynn C., Lorraine Moya Salas, Flavio F. Marsiglia, Scott T. Yabiku, Blythe Fitzharris, and Kelly F. Jackson. 2009. "Youths of Mexican Descent of the Southwest: Exploring Differences in Ethnic Labels." *Children and Schools* 31 (1): 15–26.

Hollinger, David A. 1995. *Postethnic America: Beyond Multiculturalism*. New York: Basic Books.

Huntington, Samuel. 2004. "The Hispanic Challenge." *Foreign Policy* 141 (2): 30–45.

Innis-Jiménez, Michael. 2013. *Steel Barrio: The Great Mexican Migration to South Chicago, 1915–1940*. New York: New York University Press.

Itzigsohn, José 2004. "The Formation of Latino and Latina Panethnicity Identity." In *Not Just Black and White: Immigration, Race, and Ethnicity, Then to Now*, edited by Nancy Foner and George Fredrickson, 197–216. New York: Russell Sage Foundation.

———. 2009. *Encountering American Faultlines: Class, Race, and the Dominican Experience*. New York: Russell Sage Foundation

Itzigsohn, José, and Carlos Dore-Cabral. 2000. "Competing Identities: Race, Ethnicity and Panethnicity among Dominicans in the United States." *Sociological Forum* 15 (2): 225–47.

Jiménez, Tomás R. 2004. "Negotiating Ethnic Boundaries: Multiethnic Mexican Americans and Ethnic Identity in the United States." *Ethnicities* 4 (1): 75–97.

———. 2010. *Replenished Ethnicity: Mexican Americans, Immigration, and Identity*. Berkeley: University of California Press.

Jones-Correa, Michael, and David Leal. 1996. "Becoming 'Hispanic': Secondary Panethnic Identification among Latin American–Origin Populations in the United States." *Hispanic Journal of Behavioral Sciences* 18 (2): 214–54.

Keeter, Scott. 2010. "Millennials: A Portrait of Generation Next." Pew Research Center. Pew Research Social and Demographic Trends. www.pewsocialtrends.org.

Kibria, Nazli. 2002. *Becoming Asian American: Identities of Second-Generation Chinese and Korean Americans*. Baltimore: Johns Hopkins University Press.

Kim, Claire Jean. 1999. "The Racial Triangulation of Asian Americans." *Politics and Society* 27:105–38.

Lee, Jennifer, and Frank Bean. 2010. *The Diversity Paradox: Immigration and the Color Line in 21st Century America*. New York: Russell Sage Foundation Press.

Lipsitz, George. 2011. *How Racism Takes Place*. Philadelphia: Temple University Press.

Lopez, Iris. 2008. *Matters of Choice: Puerto Rican Women's Struggle for Reproductive Freedom*. New Brunswick, NJ: Rutgers University Press.

López, Nancy. 2002. *Hopeful Girls, Troubled Boys: Race and Gender Disparity in Urban Education*. New York: Routledge.

Massey, Douglas S., and Magaly Sanchez R. 2010. *Brokered Boundaries: Immigrant Identity in Anti-immigrant Times*. New York: Russell Sage Foundation.

Masuoka, Natalie. 2006. "Together They Become One: Examining the Predictors of Panethnic Group Consciousness among Asian Americans and Latinos." *Social Science Quarterly* 87 (5): 993–1011.

McConnell, Eileen Diaz, and Edward A. Delgado-Romero. 2004. "Latino Panethnicity: Reality or Methodological Construction?" *Sociological Focus* 37 (4): 297–312.

MacDonald, Victoria-Maria. 2004. *Latino Education in the United States: A Narrated History from 1513–2000*. New York: Palgrave Macmillan.

Menchaca, Martha. 2002. *Recovering History, Constructing Race: The Indian, Black, and White Roots of Mexican Americans*. Austin: University of Texas Press.

Molina, Natalia. 2014. *How Race Is Made in America: Immigration, Citizenship, and the Historical Power of Racial Scripts*. Berkeley: University of California Press.

Mora, G. Cristina. 2014a. "Cross-Field Effects and Ethnic Classification: The Institutionalization of Hispanic Panethnicity." *American Sociological Review* 79 (2): 183–210.

———. 2014b. *Making Hispanics: How Activists, Bureaucrats, and Media Constructed a New American*. Chicago: University of Chicago Press.

Morning, Ann. 2009. "Toward a Sociology of Racial Conceptualization for the 21st Century." *Social Forces* 87 (3): 1–26.

———. 2011. *The Nature of Race: How Scientists Think and Teach about Human Difference*. Berkeley: University of California Press.

Munoz, Carlos. 2007. *Youth, Identity, Power: The Chicano Movement*. 2nd revised and expanded edition. New York: Verso.

Murguia, Edward, and Tyrone Forman. 2003. "Shades of Whiteness: The Mexican American Experience in Relation to Anglos and Blacks." In *Whiteout: The Continuing Significance of Racism*, edited by Woody Doane and Eduardo Bonilla-Silva, 63–79. New York: Routledge.

Murguia, Edward, and Rogelio Saenz. 2002. "An Analysis of the Latin Americanization of Race in the United States: A Reconnaissance of Color Stratification among Mexicans." *Race and Society* 5:85–101.

National Center on Citizenship. 2013. *Millennials Civil Health Index*. www.ncoc.net.

Ngai, Mae M. 2004. *Impossible Subjects: Illegal Aliens and the Making of Modern America*. Princeton, NJ: Princeton University Press.

———. 2007. "Birthright Citizenship and the Alien Citizen." *Fordham Law Review* 75 (1): 2521–30.

Oboler, Suzanne. 1992. "The Politics of Labeling: Latino/a Cultural Identities of Self and Others." *Latin American Perspectives* 19 (4): 18–36.

———. 1995. *Ethnic Labels, Latino Lives: Identity and the Politics of (Re)Presentation in the United States*. Minneapolis: University of Minnesota Press.

O'Brien. Eileen. 2008. *The Racial Middle: Latinos and Asian Americans Living beyond the Racial Divide*. New York: New York University Press.

Omi, Michael, and Howard Winant. 2014. *Racial Formation in the United States*. 3rd ed. New York: Routledge.

Padilla, Elena. 1947. "Puerto Rican immigrants in New York and Chicago: A Study in Comparative Assimilation." Master's thesis, University of Chicago.

Padilla, Felix. 1985. *Latino Ethnic Consciousness: The Case of Mexican Americans and Puerto Ricans in Chicago*. South Bend, IN: Notre Dame University Press.

Pallares, Amalia, and Nilda Flores-González. 2010. "Introduction." In *Marcha! Latino Chicago and the Immigrant Rights Movement*, edited by Amalia Pallares and Nilda Flores-González, xv–xxix. Urbana: University of Illinois Press.

Park, Edward J. W., and John S. W. Park. 1999. "A New American Dilemma? Asian Americans and Latinos in Race Theorizing." *Journal of Asian American Studies* 2 (3): 289–309.

Pascale, Celine-Marie. 2008. "Talking about Race: Shifting the Analytical Paradigm." *Qualitative Inquiry* 14 (5): 723–41.

Perea, Juan F. 1997. *Immigrants Out! The New Nativism and the Anti-immigrant Impulse in the United States*. New York: New York University Press.

Perez, Anthony Daniel, and Charles Hirschman. 2009. "The Changing Racial and Ethnic Composition of the US Population: Emerging American Identities." *Population and Development Review* 35 (1): 1–51.

Pérez, Gina. 2003. *The Near Northwest Side Story: Migration, Displacement, and Puerto Rican Families*. Berkeley: University of California Press.

———. 2015. *Citizen, Student, Soldier: Latina/o Youth, JROTC, and the American Dream*. New York: New York University Press.

Pew Hispanic Center. 2009. "Between Two Worlds: How Young Latinos Come of Age in America." Washington, DC. www.pewhispanic.org.

———. 2010. "Table 1: Chicago, IL, Metropolitan Area, Characteristics of the Population by Race, Ethnicity and Nativity." Washington, DC. www.pewhispanic.org.

Pew Research Center. 2014. "Millennials in Adulthood: Detached from Institutions, Networked with Friends." Washington, DC. www.pewsocialtrends.org.

———. 2015. "Multiracial in America: Proud, Diverse and Growing in Numbers." Washington, DC. www.pewsocialtrends.org.

Phinney, Jean. 1996. "When We Talk about American Ethnic Groups, What Do We Mean?" *American Psychologist* 51 (9): 918–27.

Pierce, Chester M., J. Carew, D. Pierce-Gonzalez, and D. Willis, D. 1978. "An Experiment in Racism: TV Commercials." In *Television and Education*, edited by C. Pierce, 62–88. Beverly Hills, CA: Sage.

Portes, Alejandro, and Ruben G. Rumbaut. 1996. *Immigrant America: A Portrait*. Berkeley: University of California Press

———. 2001. *Legacies: The Story of the Immigrant Second Generation*. Berkeley: University of California Press.

Portes, Alejandro, and Min Zhou. 1993. "The New Second Generation: Segmented Assimilation and Its Variants." *Annals of the American Academy of Political and Social Sciences* 530:74–96.

Prewitt, Kenneth. 2013. *What Is "Your" Race? The Census and Our Flawed Efforts to Classify Americans*. Princeton, NJ: Princeton University Press.

Ready, Timothy, and Allert Brown-Gort. 2005. *The State of Latino Chicago: This Is Home Now*. Institute for Latino Studies, University of Notre Dame. latinostudies.nd.edu.

Ricourt, Milagros, and Ruby Danta. 2003. *Hispanas de Queens: Latino Panethnicity in a New York City Neighborhood*. Ithaca, NY: Cornell University Press.

Rios, Victor. 2011. *Punished: Policing the Lives of Black and Latino Boys*. New York: New York University Press.

Rivera-Servera, R. 2012. *Performing Queer Latinidad: Dance, Sexuality, Politics*. Ann Arbor: University of Michigan Press.

Rodriguez, Clara. 1997. *Latin Looks: Images of Latinas and Latinos in the U.S. Media*. Boulder, CO: Westview Press.

———. 2000. *Changing Race: Latinos, the Census, and the History of Ethnicity in the United States*. New York: New York University Press.

Rodriguez, Clara, Michael Miyawani, and Gregory Aergeros. 2013. "Latino Racial Reporting in the US: To Be or Not to Be." *Sociological Compass* 4:1–14.

Rodríguez-Muñíz, Michael. 2010. "Grappling with Latinidad: Puerto Rican Activism in Chicago's Pro-Immigrant Activism." In *Marcha! Latino Chicago and the Immigrant Rights Movement*, edited by Amalia Pallares and Nilda Flores-González, 237–58. Urbana: University of Illinois Press.

———. 2015. "The Politics of the Future: Demographic Knowledge, Latino/a Spokespersons, and the 'Browning of America.'" PhD diss., Brown University.

Rosa, Jonathan. 2014. "Nuevo Chicago? Language, Diaspora, and Latina/o Panethnic Formations." In *A Sociolinguistics of Diaspora: Latino Practices, Identities, and Ideologies*, edited by Rosina Marquez and Luisa Martín Rojo, 31–47. New York: Routledge.

———. 2016a. "Racializing Language, Regimenting Latinas/os: Chronotope, Social Tense, and American Raciolinguistic Futures." *Language and Communication* 46:106–17.

———. 2016b. "Standardization, Racialization, Languagelessness: Raciolinguistic Ideologies across Communicative Contexts." *Journal of Linguistic Anthropology* 26 (2): 162–83.

Rosaldo, Renato. 1997. "Cultural Citizenship, Inequality, Multiculturalism." In *Latino Cultural Citizenship: Claiming Identity, Space, and Rights*, edited by William Flores and Rina Benmayor, 27–38. Boston: Beacon Press.

Rosaldo, Renato, and William Flores. 1997. "Identity, Conflict, and Evolving Latino Communities: Cultural Citizenship in San José, California." In *Latino Cultural Citizenship: Claiming Identity, Space, and Rights*, edited by William Flores and Rina Benmayor, 57–98. Boston: Beacon Press.

Roth, Wendy D. 2012. *Race Migrations: Latinos and the Cultural Transformation of Race*. Palo Alto, CA: Stanford University Press.

Rúa, Mérida. 2001. "Colao Subjectivities: PortoMex and MexiRican Perspectives on Language and Identity." *CENTRO: Journal of the Center for Puerto Rican Studies* 13 (2): 116–33.

———, ed. 2010. *Latino Urban Ethnography and the Work of Elena Padilla*. Urbana: University of Illinois Press.

———. 2012. *A Grounded Latinidad: Making New Lives in Chicago's Puerto Rican Neighborhoods*. New York: Oxford University Press.

Rumbaut, Ruben. 1994. "The Crucible Within: Ethnic Identity, Self-Esteem, and Segmented Assimilation among Children of Immigrants." *International Migration Review* 28 (4): 748–94.

Santa Ana, Otto. 2002. *Brown Tide Rising: Metaphors of Latinos in Contemporary American Public Discourse*. Austin: University of Texas Press.

Schildkraut, Deborah. 2011. *Americanism in the Twenty-First Century: Public Opinion in the Age of Immigration*. Cambridge: Cambridge University Press.

Schmidt, Ronald, Edwina Barvosa-Carter, and Rodolfo D. Torres. 2000. "Latina/o Identities: Social Diversity and U.S. Politics." *PS: Political Science and Politics* 33 (3): 563–67.

Sears, David O., and Victoria Savalei. 2006. "The Political Color Line in America: Many Peoples of Color or Black Exceptionalism?" *Political Psychology* 27:895–924.

Silvestrini, Blanca. 1997. "The World We Enter When Claiming Rights: Latinos and the Quest for Culture." In *Latino Cultural Citizenship: Claiming Identity, Space, and Rights*, edited by William V. Flores and R. Benmayor, 39–57. Boston: Beacon Press.

Sledge, Matt. 2011. "Chicago Latino Population Spreads to Suburbs, Presenting New Regional Challenges." *Huffington Post*, October 10. www.huffingtonpost.com.

Smith, Rogers M. 1988. "The 'American Creed' and American Identity: The Limits of Liberal Citizenship in the United States." *Western Political Quarterly* 41 (2): 225–51.

Suarez-Orozco, Carola. 2015. *Transitions: The Development of Children of Immigrants*. New York: New York University Press.

Tafoya, Sonya. 2004. "Shades of Belonging." Washington, DC: Pew Hispanic Center. December 6. www.pewhispanic.org.

Takaki, Ronald. 1989. *Strangers from a Different Shore: A History of Asian Americans*. Boston: Little, Brown.

Taylor, Paul, Mark Hugo Lopez, Jessica Hamar Martinez, and Gabriel Velasco. 2012. "When Labels Don't Fit: Hispanics and Their Views of Identity." Washington, DC: Pew Hispanic Center. www.pewhispanic.org.

Telles, Edward E., and Vilma Ortiz. 2008. *Generations of Exclusion: Mexican Americans, Assimilation, and Race*. New York: Russell Sage Foundation.

Theiss-Morse, Elizabeth. 2009. *Who Counts as an American? The Boundaries of National Identity*. Cambridge: Cambridge University Press.

Torres-Saillant, Silvio. 2003. "Inventing the Race: Latinos and the Ethnoracial Pentagon." *Latino Studies* 1 (1): 123–51.

Tsuda, Takeyuki. 2014. "'I'm American, Not Japanese!': The Struggle for Racial Citizenship among Later-Generation Japanese Americans." *Ethnic and Racial Studies* 37 (3): 631–49.

Tuan, Mia. 1999. *Forever Foreigners or Honorary Whites? The Asian Ethnic Experience Today*. New Brunswick, NJ: Rutgers University Press.

Urciuoli, Bonnie. 1998. *Exposing Prejudice: Puerto Rican Experiences of Language, Race, and Class*. New York: Westview Press.

U.S. Census Bureau. 2011. "Overview of Race and Hispanic Origin: 2010." www.census.gov.

———. 2012. "Results from the 2010 Census Race and Hispanic Origin Alternative Questionnaire Experiment." www.census.gov.

———. 2013. "State & County Quick Facts." www.census.gov.

Valencia, Richard. 1991. *Chicano School Failure and Success: Past, Present, and Future*. New York: Routledge.

Vallejo, Jody Agius. 2012. *Barrios to Burbs: The Making of the Mexican American Middle Class*. Stanford, CA: Stanford University Press.

Varsanyi, Monica. 2010. *Taking Local Control: Immigration Policy Activism in U.S. Cities and States*. Palo Alto, CA: Stanford University Press.

Vasquez, Jessica. 2010. "Blurred Borders for Some but Not 'Others': Gender, Racialization, Flexible Ethnicity and Third-Generation Mexican American Identity." *Sociological Perspectives* 53 (1): 45–71.

———. 2011. *Mexican Americans across Generations: Immigrant Families, Racial Realities*. New York: New York University Press.

Vega, Sugey. 2015. *Latino Heartland: Of Borders and Belonging in the Midwest*. New York: New York University Press.

Voss, Kim, and Irene Bloemraad, eds. 2011. *Rallying for Immigrant Rights: The Fight for Inclusion in 21st Century America*. Berkeley: University of California Press.

Walter, Nicholas. 2015. *The DREAMers: How the Undocumented Youth Movement Transformed the Immigrant Rights Debate*. Palo Alto, CA: Stanford University Press.

Warren, Jonathan W., and France Winddance Twine. 1997. "White Americans, the New Minority? Non-blacks and the Ever-Expanding Boundaries of Whiteness." *Journal of Black Studies* 28 (2): 200–218.

Yancey, George. 2003. *Who Is White? Latinos, Asians and the New Black/NonBlack Divide*. Boulder, CO: Lynne Rienner.

Zhou, Min. 1997. "Segmented Assimilation: Issues, Controversies, and Recent Research on the New Second Generation." *International Migration Review* 31 (4): 975–1008.

INDEX

ABOUT THE AUTHOR

Nilda Flores-González is Professor of Sociology at the University of Illinois at Chicago. Her publications include *School Kids/Street Kids: Identity Development in Latino Students* and two co-edited books: *Marcha! Latino Chicago and the Immigrant Rights Movement* and *Immigrant Women in the Neoliberal Era*.

DEC 2017

CPSIA information can be obtained
at www.ICGtesting.com
Printed in the USA
LVOW07s0517021217
558279LV00026B/230/P

9 781479 840779